100 Ways to Beat the Blues

TANYA TUCKER
AND Friends

A FIRESIDE BOOK

Published by Simon & Schuster

New York   London   Toronto   Sydney

FIRESIDE
Rockefeller Center
1230 Avenue of the Americas
New York, NY 10020

This Fireside Edition 2006

"Happiness" by Wesley McNair and "The Universal Joint" by Daniel Wolff
are reprinted with permission of McNair and Wolff.

"Midnight with Jimmy Scott," lyrics by Joe Pellitteri. Permission by Joe Pellitteri.

"Watchin' the Rain," words and music by Delbert McClinton, Nasty Cat Music
(BMI). Permission by Delbert McClinton.

FIRESIDE and colophon are registered trademarks
of Simon & Schuster, Inc.

For information about special discounts for bulk purchases,
please contact Simon & Schuster Special Sales at
1-800-456-6798 or business@simonandschuster.com.

Designed by Jill Webber

Manufactured in the United States of America

10   9   8   7   6   5   4   3   2   1

The Library of Congress has cataloged the hardcover edition as follows:
  100 ways to beat the blues / Tanya Tucker and friends.
      p. cm.
    "A Fireside Book."
    1. Melancholy—Miscellanea. 2. Celebrities—Psychology—Miscellanea. I. Title:
  One hundred ways to beat the blues. II. Tucker, Tanya.
  BF575.M44A15 2005
  152.4—dc22   2004065347

ISBN-13: 978-0-7432-7018-2
ISBN-10:   0-7432-7018-5
ISBN-13: 978-0-7432-8285-7 (Pbk.)
ISBN-10:   0-7432-8285-X (Pbk.)

THIS BOOK IS DEDICATED TO THE BEST THREE WAYS

I EVER FOUND TO BEAT THE BLUES: MY CHILDREN,

Presley, Grayson, and Layla.

Acknowledgments

My first thank-you must go to author Cathie Pelletier, who is also the agent for this book. Cathie was sitting on her patio with the Sunday blues when she thought up the idea for *100 Ways to Beat the Blues*. She immediately brought the concept to my friend and biographer, Patsi Bale Cox, and me. We both fell in love with the idea. Cathie started asking some of her friends in music and literary circles how they coped with "down times," and Patsi and I started doing the same. Right away we could see that people from all walks of life certainly share an understanding of the blues, and have lots of ways of battling them!

Responses ranged from funny and light to poignant and practical. And sometimes, the blues were, well, heavier for some folks, as you will read.

We were fortunate to find a like-minded editor in Trish Todd at Fireside (a former Nashvillian to boot), who saw the book's potential and gave us the opportunity to publish our findings. Trish, as well as art director Cherlynne Li, senior production editor Tricia Wygal, publicity director Marcia Burch, deputy publisher Chris Lloreda, and publisher Mark Gompertz, has welcomed us like family. The entire Fireside team has been a joy to work with. No blues at our new publishing home!

Our aim was always to include people from a wide range of backgrounds and professions, and to that end, we enlisted help from some other great folks. We give our thanks to Connie Nelson, Jack Fox, John Lappen and Paradise Entertainment, Mona Orvig, Tom Viorikic, Danny Gadarian, Shad Meshad, Ken Onstad, and Becky Richardson. A very special thank-you to all the participants who took the time to tell us how they beat the blues. Without them, this book would not have been possible.

And last, but certainly not least, thanks to my family, always there and always supportive.

Contents

I've never seen a guy so green have the blues so bad.

—ROWLF THE DOG, ABOUT KERMIT THE FROG,

The Muppet Movie, 1979

1 The Two-Hour Blues

TANYA TUCKER

Any entertainer will tell you that when you get on that tour bus, you sometimes feel you are leaving the problems of the real world behind. You're out there on the road where problems with the plumbing at your house, or the lawn that needs mowing, or the important call you haven't returned are miles away. They'll usually be waiting for you upon your return, but still, it's out of sight, out of mind. But the one thing you can't outrun on the road is the blues. The blues travel fast. They'll catch up.

Getting up onstage and feeling the love of your fans goes a long ways toward holding the blues at bay out there on the road. So does getting a call from an old friend, listening to the radio and hearing a great song, or discovering a new artist whose music you love. The sound of rain on the bus's roof always cheers me up. Sometimes, if it's raining when I come in off the road, I linger on the bus a little longer—not to stay out of the rain, just to hear that pitter-patter sound on the roof.

But other times you have to reach down inside yourself and really come up with a powerful solution to the blues. In my case, inspiration comes from my family. My children, of course, always bring me up. A hug, a smile, an "I love you, Mom." And then, I can always look to my parents, to their lives and strengths.

Mother and Daddy came up poor and proud, and raised me to believe in myself, no matter how bad things looked. In the late 1930s, my mother's family, the Cunninghams, moved from Abilene, Texas, to work on a ranch near the New Mexico border, in Gains County, Texas. They worked with the horses and cattle, picked cotton, and tended to the watermelon patches. Then the ranch owners struck oil, and, like so many other Texans, Mother's family started working in the oil fields. It was there that Mother met my father, Beau Tucker. In 1943, the two married. Mother was fifteen years old, but from that day on, she was Daddy's support system. She packed up and moved with him as he chased work all over the Southwest.

When I was nine years old, we drove up to St. George, Utah, where Daddy had heard of jobs in construction. The jobs were there, but it was an unstable, on-again, off-again industry. At one point we were about as poor as a family could get, living in a beat-up trailer and eating government cheese. Then Daddy lost his job, Mama got sick, and we fell a hundred and fifty dollars behind on our rent. One morning Daddy cranked up his old Ford truck and went out to look for work while I stayed home from school to take care of Mama. All of a sudden, there was a knock on the door. I answered it, and two big men in suits burst into the living room and started yelling at Mama about the rent. She tried to explain that Daddy was on the verge of getting another job, but they weren't in a mood to listen. They were in a mood to kick us out.

I yelled and cried, but those men dragged Mama outside, sat her down on the curb, and padlocked the doors to that beat-up trailer. She and I stayed huddled together for two hours before Daddy got home. As it happened, he had found a job, and was able to get a small advance. He rented us a furnished room, and we had a roof over our heads again.

But for two hours I had been as lowdown as I have ever been in my life. I will always remember that feeling, knowing that for the want of a hundred and fifty dollars strangers could leave my mother in her housecoat, sick and coughing, by the side of the road and I couldn't do a damn thing about it.

I started singing professionally that same year. Four years later, at the age of thirteen, I had my first hit record. My family has never wanted for anything since. So when I get the blues over some real or imagined problem, I picture Mama on the curb in St. George, Utah. And that's when my spirits soar in the knowledge that it will never happen again.

So my advice is this: If you've got the blues, look back over your life. Think about other hard times and how you overcame them. Then give yourself a pat on the back.

I promise you'll feel better.

2 The Wrong Motorcycle Blues

ROSEANNE

Actually, I have been known to beat up on the blues. One day I took two shots of tequila, a brand-new baseball bat, and found myself staring at my ex-husband's prized motorcycle.

It was only later, after I was proudly assessing the damage, that I discovered this particular cycle was one of mine!

Oh, well, sometimes you just gotta laugh. And that'll beat the blues.

Roseanne has distinguished herself as one of entertainment's funniest ladies, along with Lucille Ball and Carol Burnett. After gaining fame as a stand-up comic, her groundbreaking show, *Roseanne*, debuted on October 18, 1988, and was number one within a year. *Roseanne* is currently viewed in syndication in 150 countries worldwide. You can visit Roseanne's website at www.roseanneworld.com.

3 Perking Up the Blues

MYRTLE TODD

I was born and raised in rural Mississippi. My parents died when I was very young, so I was sent to live with family members in the area. I had to grow up fast. Although they were good people and treated me like their own, I missed having a mother and father something awful. But even as a child, I decided that there were two ways to look at your circumstances. You could say, "Poor little me" or "I'm lucky to be alive and one of God's children."

I married young, like so many girls back in the 1920s and 1930s, and I welcomed six children to this earth. I tried to pass my belief in staying positive along to each child.

I was always a good worker, proud of being a physically strong woman. I could work on the farm right along with the men, if need be. I tried to pass along my belief in the value of hard work to my children, too. But the truth is, when you get to be as old as I am, it's difficult to do that hard work. You have to get help for this and that, and you find yourself longing for your old strength back again.

Staying positive is now something that I have to remind myself to do. I'll always be thinking of ways to keep from getting down in the dumps. My favorite remedy is music. So if I start feeling a little puny, I just pick up my old guitar and sing a few hymns.

Before I know it, I'm perked right up again.

At eighty-eight years of age, Myrtle Todd recently retired as the host of *The Senior Center Gospel Hour Radio Show*, broadcast from WPRN in Butler, Alabama. Not one to sit around for long without doing some task, she returns to the station regularly as a guest of deejay Henry Tyson.

4 Sweeping Away the Blues

GEOFF BODINE

It will come as no surprise to anyone that getting in a car and driving fast brings me out of the dumps. But that's not how I usually beat the blues. The truth is, I clean. If I get down about something, I'll polish the entire house, clean out the garage, reorganize my office, wax my car, and groom my animals. In fact, my two dogs are never brushed as much as when I'm feeling bad. I guess you could say I sweep away the blues!

Geoff Bodine is one of America's racing legends, with eighteen Winston Cup victories and thirty-seven career pole positions. He was voted one of NASCAR's Fifty Greatest Drivers in 1998. He is listed in the *Guinness Book of World Records* for having the most wins, fifty-five, in a single season, and has six Busch Grand National series wins. He won the Race of Champions for asphalt modifieds twice, and placed first in the 1986 Daytona 500, the 1987 International Race of Champions, the 1992 Busch Clash, the 1994 Winston Select, and won the 1994 Busch Pole Award.

5 How We Beat the Blues

GEORGE AND BARBARA BUSH

GEORGE: When I get down in the dumps I talk back to the TV set. I have even sworn at the TV set and yelled at the bubblehead on TV with whom I do not agree. It hurts a lot more when our son, the president, is attacked than when I used to be in the crosshairs. I expect it is of no lasting benefit when I shout at the TV, but it sure feels good at the time.

BARBARA: I do not get down in the dumps because I refuse to watch TV when the president (current and even past) is criticized. I tune out, and go about walking our dog Sadie, or working on one of my many reading projects. I understand "this too shall pass." I have many blessings to count about family, and I refuse to let critics, be they political or journalistic, get me down.

GEORGE: Speaking of "beating the blues," my mother always told me, "George, don't get down in the dumps." I never understood what "the dumps" were, but when, at age twelve, I'd lose an important match, and even later in life when I'd lose an important election, I remembered Mum's advice. "Keep your chin up. Set an example for others. Don't blame anyone else for your own shortcomings. And when you win, remember the guy you beat. Don't gloat or be arrogant. He will be hurting, so be kind." Even when I was president, I remembered her valuable advice.

BARBARA: I guess the hardest thing for me was way back in the early fifties, when our little four-year-old daughter died of leukemia. I was devastated, as was George. I sat by her bed and watched her suffer. Then, I watched her at peace as she went to heaven. I found that prayer helped enormously. I always wondered why our lovely, innocent four-year-old was taken off to heaven so early in her life. But prayer helped me understand God's will. Prayer lifted me up and helped me get on with the life that has been so fulfilling for both George and me.

George Herbert Walker Bush served as the forty-first president of the United States, from 1989 to 1993. Former first lady Barbara Bush is the author of several books, including *Barbara Bush: A Memoir*.

6 The Finite Blues

SIR ARTHUR C. CLARKE

I very seldom suffer from the blues.
But on those rare occasions, I have
had two infallible remedies:

1. Exploring the infinite universe of fractals.
2. Playing with my killer Chihuahua, Dainty.

Sir Arthur C. Clarke is the author of more than seventy books. His many honors include doctorates in science and literature, the Gold Medal of the Franklin Institute, the Marconi Fellowship, the Charles A. Lindbergh Award, the UNESCO-Kalinga Prize, the Distinguished Public Service Medal (NASA's highest civilian award), and the Special Achievement Medal of the Association of Space Explorers. His screenplay for *2001: A Space Odyssey* (directed by Stanley Kubrick) was nominated for an Oscar in 1968.

7 On the Road Blues

JAMES GREGORY

Years ago, when I was out on the road playing clubs, not making much money, and spending a lot of time alone, I'd start to get filled with self-doubt. I'd wonder what I was doing way out in Oklahoma, earning around $250 a week and having to pay my expenses out of it. I'd go down to the local Waffle House and order a grilled cheese sandwich and a glass of water because I couldn't afford anything else.

I don't call what I was going through the blues. I call it feeling sorry for myself. And as time went by I learned what I had to do to snap myself out of it. I have a serious conversation with myself. You can do the same, whether you are in a diner in Tulsa, Oklahoma, or a mall in Brockton, Massachusetts.

My conversation with me starts out with a calculation of the number of hospitals within ten to fifteen miles of where I am. I remind myself that there are thousands of sick people in those hospitals. Some of those people are going to come out of the hospitals missing an arm or a leg. Some will be released without hope. Some won't come out alive.

What that means is that within a few miles of where I am, there are thousands of people who would trade places with me in a second.

By the time I'm that far into the conversation with myself, I stop feeling depressed and start to feel guilty.

I may be ordering a glass of sweet tea in a Tulsa diner, or buying socks in that mall in Brockton, but in my mind I'm saying: I've got a job I like most of the time. I've got family. I've got friends. I'm pretty healthy.

I'll think about that waitress in the diner, who may have just worked a double shift to support her kids, or the person selling socks at the mall who may be worried about some tests the doctor just ran. Then I say a silent prayer that God will forgive me for whining, and remind Him to keep paying attention to those who really need Him.

Then I say this: The sun is gonna come up tomorrow. It always does. Winter will go, and spring will appear. Dogwood and honeysuckle will bloom again.

Billed as "the Funniest Man in America," stand-up comic James Gregory plays standing-room-only shows forty-nine weeks a year. He recorded an acclaimed Epic Records album, *It Could Be a Law, I Don't Know*, and more recently, *Grease, Gravy, and John Wayne's Momma*. You can visit his website at www.funniestman.com.

8 An Alternative to the Blues

WILLIE NELSON

If you don't like the blues, play from the whites.

In a career spanning more than four decades, Willie Nelson has become one of the most recognized entertainment icons in American history. He organized the annual Farm Aid benefit concerts starting in 1985, received the ACM's Pioneer Award in 1991, was inducted into the Country Music Hall of Fame in 1993, and was fêted at the Kennedy Center Honors in 1998. You can visit his website at www.willienelson.com.

9 The Walter Mitty Blues

ROBERT TIMMERMAN

Do I get the blues? I work in a factory, doing twelve-hour shifts, making radial truck tires for eighteen-wheelers. Is it snowing out today? Raining? Is the wind blowing? There's no way to tell when you're doing factory work.

Had anyone told me thirty years ago that I would still be earning a living this way, I would have told them they obviously had me confused with some other drone. Not a chance. Thirty years ago I was on the cusp of writing the Great American Novel, after which I would retire to a comfortable cabin in the mountains with my fly rod and a sedate Labrador retriever. But, of course, that was before I had decided to major in beer and tennis, instead of journalism or premed. At some point during that critical stage of my life it must have seemed like a good idea to drop out of school for a few months and put aside some money for a serious reentry into college.

That six-month respite from school has since morphed into thirty years of relentless, mind-numbing tedium on a factory floor. One might call that decision a career error. I know I certainly do. It seems like overnight I went from "young man with potential" to "father nearing retirement." One day you're hauling a kid to his T-ball practice, and the next day some smirking jerk is handing you a gold watch and thanking you for having been such a productive "associate" for all of those years.

The reality of a check-to-check existence on a factory payroll is enough to give anyone the blues. Twelve-hour shifts on concrete floors, deprived of any contact or view of the outside world, can make even the best of days seem dreary. Everyone in that environment has his or her own way of coping with the repetitious, physical work, and the stifling sense of imprisonment that production work demands.

So how do you beat it? My own escape mechanism has always been the fine art of daydreaming. If you can't actually wade out into a clear mountain stream with a fly rod in hand to spend the afternoon making lazy casts into the pools beneath the rapids, a well-crafted daydream can be almost as therapeutic. I've spent countless hours on a clothing-optional beach at a Jamaican resort, all the while churning out tire after tire and rolling them to the conveyor belt. Some days, I see myself finally settling down at a quiet desk, with a good typewriter and plenty of paper, to write that Great American Novel.

I'll leave it to the psychologists to determine if thirty years in a Walter Mitty haze is healthy or delusional. All I know is that when you can't change your reality, sometimes it helps to change your *perception* of that reality. Now, if you'll excuse me, I think I see a fat rainbow trout rising in the shallows below the spillway. No license required, and no limit.

Robert Timmerman lives in Nashville, Tennessee, and works in a tire factory.

10 The Faces of the Blues

GAYLE SAYERS

There are many faces to the blues. They show up in a multitude of ways: problems at home, the loss of a job, illness, death. For me, there is one sure way to deal with any kind of blues: prayer. I pray for forgiveness for my sins.

Seeing Mel Gibson's *The Passion of the Christ* affected me tremendously. Any earthly blues we might get pale by comparison to what our lord and savior, Jesus Christ, went through for our sins. We are all going on home one day, to where the blues don't exist.

Chicago Bears running back Gayle Sayers is the youngest player in NFL history to be inducted into the Pro Football Hall of Fame. His friendship with fellow Chicago Bear Brian Piccolo, who was stricken with cancer, was made into a film, *Brian's Song,* in 1971. Sayers is the CEO of Illinois-based Sayers 40 Inc. You can visit his website at www.sayers.com.

11 The Backseat Blues

WESLEY MCNAIR

A while back my mother-in-law, Sue Reed, a beloved figure in my family, had a stroke that paralyzed her left side, which gave us all the blues. Our hearts sank as we watched her struggle to make the smallest movements with her leg or arm or hand. But one day, after a month of physical therapy, she was able to stand on her quadcane, and a few days later, to walk with it. All my wife, Diane, and I wanted to do then was celebrate.

So I packed my mother-in-law and her quadcane into the passenger seat of her two-door sedan, Diane got into the backseat, and I drove us to dinner. On the way, spirits high, we picked up Sue's sister, Dot, a large woman who dearly loves to eat, and soon we were pulling into the sunny parking lot of the restaurant. There, something disastrous happened. We couldn't get Dot out of the backseat. No matter how much we pushed and prodded and rocked her, she was lodged back there.

Surely, Dear Reader, you have noticed that just when you think you have escaped trouble and the blues, the two return to threaten you again. Here is a poem I wrote about how Dot got out of the car and the rest of us escaped the blues a second time. So, next time you get the blues, take a lesson from Dot. Instead of just sitting there, reach out to those who love you for help.

Happiness

Why, Dot asks, stuck in the backseat
of her sister's two-door, her freckled hand
feeling the roof for the right spot
to pull her wide self up onto her left,
the unarthritic, ankle—why
does her sister, coaching outside on her cane,
have to make her laugh so, she flops
back just as she was, though now,
looking wistfully out through the restaurant
reflected in her back window, she seems bigger,
and couldn't possibly mean we should go
ahead in without her, she'll be all right, and so

when you finally place the pillow behind her back
and lift her right out into the sunshine,
all four of us are happy, none more
than she, who straightens the blossoms
on her blouse, says how nice it is to get out
once in a while, and then goes in to eat
with the greatest delicacy (oh,
I could never finish all that) and aplomb
the complete roast beef dinner with apple crisp
and ice cream, just a small scoop.

Wes McNair is the author of seven collections of poetry and editor of two anthologies of contemporary writing. He is the recipient of fellowships from the Rockefeller, Fulbright, and Guggenheim foundations; several grants from the National Endowment for the Arts; and numerous awards, including the Robert Frost Prize, the Devins Award for Poetry, and the Theodore Roethke Prize. Visit him at www.wesleymcnair.com.

12 The Late-Night Blues

LORETTA LYNN

Sometimes when I'm not on tour, I rattle around my new house in Hurricane Mills, Tennessee, and start thinking about my husband, Doolittle Lynn. He was the reason I got into the music business in the first place, and he's the reason I stayed through good times and bad. He died in 1996 and I've missed him every day since.

Sometimes I get up in the middle of the night and walk down the road to the old antebellum home where we first moved, the one that came with bad flooring and Civil War ghosts. Nobody but the ghosts lives there anymore. That's when I get to thinking about how hard Doo worked getting the old place fixed up, and before I know it, I'm real down in the dumps. But then I think about how tough my husband was, how nothing kept him down for long. And I tell myself that if Doolittle Lynn was standing there with me, he'd get gruff as an old bear:

"Loretta, get yourself out of the night air, fix yourself a fried baloney sandwich, and say to hell with the blues!"

So that's what I do.

Loretta Lynn is one of the greatest stars of country music. *Coal Miner's Daughter*, her bestselling life story, became an award-winning film of the same title. You can visit her website at www.lorettalynn.com.

13 The Broken Heart Blues

IAN DUNCAN

I wonder if I'll be the only person in this book who is blue because of love? The only one with a broken heart? One of my favorite songs says that to love someone is the greatest thing we'll ever know. That, and to be loved in return. It's not as easy as it sounds, although it should be.

My career is enough to make me blue now and then. I'm an actor, and an actor's life is constantly surrounded by insecurities, struggles, heartache, and rejection. Emotions are extreme. The highs are HIGH, and the lows are DEEP. The exhilaration I feel when shooting a film is indescribable. It's the "in between jobs" period when I feel most vulnerable, even sorry for myself.

Ambition made me leave Cape Town, South Africa, where I was born. My family and my oldest friends are all still there. I split my time these days between London and Los Angeles, both places very different from where I grew up. It's harder to have the blues in L.A. than in London because the sun shines so much in California. At times, with the sun rising, breathing life on a new day, I find my old self, the part of me that is constantly happy and positive.

I often wonder what my life would be like if I had a regular nine-to-five job. I think I would probably be happily married, with a family, and still living in Cape Town. But whatever pumps through my veins, whatever drives me to be an actor, tells me to keep going. Do I suffer from too much ambition? Probably.

This brings me to my broken heart and the blues. I was involved with an incredible woman for seven years. I loved her a lot. But love often takes a backseat to acting, especially when ambition is necessary for success. If this were a script, I'd say, "It's a modern-day *Romeo and Juliet* love story." We still love each other, and yet our lives are unfurling in opposite directions. Shakespeare once said that "love is not love which alters when it alteration finds," but there's a lot of alteration in my life and our love couldn't survive the changes.

So, anyone out there with the "broken heart blues," whether your story is like mine, or whether you're going through divorce, or whether your relationship just broke down at the side of the road and won't go any further, you understand what I'm feeling. I do believe that time can heal all wounds, but what I want to know is this: How long does it take for a broken heart to mend?

Here's what I do know. I know that I am blessed, for I have wonderful friends and a loving family. And they don't seem to mind if I happen to be wearing my heart right there on my sleeve. Will I read this ten years from now and be thankful?

Will I see that it forced me to take a path that brought me even more happiness in life? I haven't got a clue. Right now it hurts. I guess it's all just a matter of time.

Ian Duncan is an actor. His credits include the role of John in the 2000 miniseries *Jesus*, and that of Brutus in the 2002 miniseries *Julius Caesar*.

14   Two Words for the Blues

ERIC BURDON

Sing 'em!

Eric Burdon is one of the seminal figures of the 1960s British Invasion. As lead singer of the legendary Animals, his gritty, blues-drenched vocals have defined such classics as "Don't Let Me Be Misunderstood," "It's My Life," "We Gotta Get Out of This Place," and his signature song, "House of the Rising Sun."

15 The Army Blues

JAMES GORDON BENNETT

As a teenager and an army brat (in every sense of the word), I would often lounge around our quarters (i.e., the house), down in the dumps about dependent life in the military. I was sick of all the curfews and regulations, the pathetically understocked commissary, the PX's back-to-school fashions that made Sears look like Versace, the perpetually running John Wayne double feature at the grungy post theater, and everywhere the alien acronyms: TDY, PCS, MOS, ad nauseam.

My father was an Airborne Ranger who didn't suffer sullen teenagers lightly: "Get up off your derriere and do something productive or I'll give you something to sulk about." And because it was a DO (direct order) from the CO (commanding officer) himself, I would snap out of my funk WFA (without further ado).

These days the old man's no longer in the chain of command and remains content to fade away in his Florida retirement condo. But he has a couple of grandsons: one just out of his teens and the other just slouching into them. Whenever, as a writer, I get to sulking about things, like my books being OOP (out of print), I try to recall how the colonel would en-

courage his sullen little soldier to get off his fanny and con-
tribute something to the greater good. It cheers me up to know
that at least for the time being I'm in charge of two occasion-
ally sullen dependents of my own. And like father, like son,
RHIP (rank has its privileges).

James Gordon Bennett is named for his great-uncle, the famed newspa-
perman who sent Stanley to find Livingstone. The author of *My Father's
Geisha* and *The Moon Stops Here*, Bennett is currently teaching at LSU and
working on a new novel.

16 The Front Porch Blues

RODNEY AMMONS

My cure for the blues is almost always the same. It's the front porch solution. Specifically, my mother's front porch. There's something timeless and reassuring in sitting with family on the porch, maybe having a glass of lemonade and a piece of pie.

People drive by and wave. Neighbors might stop in to talk about the weather. The blues aren't allowed. In fact, I think it's against the law for the blues to follow you up on your mother's front porch!

Rodney Ammons is a bootmaker in Nashville, Tennessee.

17 The Blues and Richard Harris

EVA JUEL

The Irish love to tell a good story, and no Irishman was better at it than Richard Harris. I was lucky enough to work as his assistant and travel with him for many years. I got to hear a lot of good stories on the set, in between takes. Sometimes, magic wands floated through the air *(Harry Potter)* or the scorching Mexican sun beat down on us all *(The Pearl)* or Richard would be clad in armor *(Julius Caesar),* but no matter: Richard still found the time to tell a good story. Sometimes, he would make himself laugh so hard that his eyes would fill with tears. "Ah, Jesus wept," he'd say, as he finished the tale.

We lost Richard in the autumn of 2002, much too soon, for with him went a great and irreplaceable talent. There were so many more important roles he could have played, and there were so many more wild stories he could have told. His family and friends will never fill the space that he left behind.

Sometimes, when the phone rings, I think it's Richard and we're off on some new film adventure. That's when the reality of losing him, the real blues, hits me hard. The only thing I can do at moments like that is to remember him fully, his funny stories and his infectious laughter.

My favorite story of all is one I'll share with you, and one that Richard loved to tell. It was during the filming of *Mutiny on the Bounty,* with Marlon Brando. Richard had arrived in Tahiti in late 1961 and was put up in a hut when the rains hit hard and filming had to stop. This was the film that Richard liked to say almost turned him into "a drunk and a tramp." Filming finally began, and, as the story goes, Brando was driving everyone insane on the set. He wanted to talk out each scene to the point of exhaustion and boredom for the cast and the director. Richard always said that he felt in his bones he and Brando would clash in some way.

Finally, it was time for their fight scene. Brando was to hit Richard so hard it would send him flying into a campfire, but instead he would deliver his lines and then give Richard a light tap on the face. Therefore, Richard stood his ground firmly, refusing to move. "I'll fall down when he hits me hard enough that it looks real," he told Lewis Milestone, the frustrated director, who had replaced the first frustrated director, Sir Carol Reed. On it went like this. Brando being Brando, he refused to hit Richard with anything more than a light tap. Finally, instead of falling into the campfire, Richard moved in quickly and kissed Brando on the face. "Shall we dance?" Richard asked the temperamental star. Shooting was quickly called off.

After Richard and his wife at the time, Elizabeth, returned to Los Angeles, he was called in to reshoot some scenes. In no way did the studio want Brando and Harris back in the same room together. Richard used to tell, in that Irish lilt of his, how they filmed the death scene. "I spoke to a wooden box instead of Marlon Brando," he'd say. It was the film's last scene and Brando (as Fletcher Christian) is dying. But Brando wasn't there, so Richard had to react to the box instead. As he was about to leave the set, makeup off, he was suddenly called back. Marlon Brando himself was now there and ready to do *his* part of that scene. Richard was asked to speak his lines to Marlon, off camera, so that the great actor could react to them. Richard was so furious that he grabbed the same wooden box and slammed it down in front of Marlon's startled face.

"Talk to THAT!" Richard shouted. "I had to!"

Ah, Jesus wept. I'm laughing so hard now that I no longer feel the blues. Thank you, Richard.

Eva Juel is a film producer from Copenhagen, Denmark. She is a graduate of the American Film Institute in producing.

18 Giving Away the Blues

MORGAN FAIRCHILD

When it comes to the blues, it's always better to give than to receive.

Morgan Fairchild began her career in the CBS daytime series *Search for Tomorrow*, and went on to act in *Dallas*, as well as in *Barnaby Jones*; *Happy Days*; *The Bob Newhart Show*; *Perry Mason*; *Murder, She Wrote*; *Lois & Clark*; and *Cybill*, among others. She has starred in numerous movies, including *The Memory of Eva Ryker*, *The Initiation of Sarah*, *Concrete Cowboy*, *North & South*, *The Dream Merchant*, and *Flamingo Road*, for which she received a Golden Globe nomination. You can visit her website at www.morganfairchild.com.

19 The Waylon Blues

WENDY RODRIGUE

He was world famous, and I never knew him. But I had the feeling that I would meet him someday, that I would shake his hand and tell him I admired him, that we'd click and become friends.

Waylon Jennings is dead. On Saturday night the Grand Ole Opry dedicated their show to the outlaw. The modern superstars sang his songs and wrote new lyrics to old tunes, singing about Waylon in the same way he sang about Hank. I couldn't help but remember his loathing for these shows. Dead four days . . . the subject of an all-star tribute . . . as big a legend as if he were Hank himself. They didn't know what to do with him when he was alive, but they felt right at home making him a legend, as though he'd been dead fifty years.

I learned of Waylon's death on the radio on Valentine's Day as I stood in the utility room of our house, unpacking from ten days of Mardi Gras fun. My husband walked in from outside just after the announcement.

"George, did you hear? Waylon Jennings died."

"I knew he was sick," George said. "Diabetes. You know, they had to cut off his foot."

Then he had to join the guests who were waiting in his studio. Left alone, I began to hum a Waylon tune. I wanted to hear that voice, to know that he still lived. Buried in a stack of CDs in the kitchen, which I'd been meaning to organize since Christmas before last, I found his greatest hits. As the music started, I went back to sorting laundry.

Soon after, George touched my shoulder from behind. He held me close, and we danced quietly between the piles of clothes until we both felt better.

Good-bye, Waylon. We'll miss you.

Wendy Rodrigue is a writer from Fort Walton Beach, Florida. She has contributed to numerous books, articles, and catalogs featuring the artwork of her husband, George. They make their home in New Orleans.

20 The Helping Hand Blues

BRENDA LEE

The year 2000 marked my fiftieth year in show business.

I don't often get down, but when I do, I reflect on how blessed I've been in my life. Then I think of something I can do for someone else.

Offering a helping hand to another will lift you up faster than anything.

Brenda Lee has sold more than one hundred million records world-wide. She is a member of both the Rock and Roll Hall of Fame and the Country Music Hall of Fame. Her autobiography, *Little Miss Dynamite: The Brenda Lee Story*, was published in 2002. You can visit her website at www.brendalee.com.

21 The Dark Side Blues

DAVID PROWSE

Long before I ever donned a suit and mask and became Darth Vader in *Star Wars,* I was confined to a tuberculosis ward and classified a "crippled child." I was only thirteen and had been a budding athlete in my hometown of Bristol, England. But one morning I got out of bed to discover that my knee was swollen and painful. Doctors immediately said it was tuberculosis of the knee and sent me off to a sanatorium that clung to a dreary hilltop, fifteen miles from Bristol. Most of the boys in the ward to which I was assigned were either rheumatic heart or tuberculosis cases.

The hospital was a dark and depressing place for me. My father had already died by the time I was five, but my mother still managed to take the bus out to visit me twice a week. It was expensive and time-consuming for her, but she always did it without complaint and with a smile to greet me. Although the tests kept coming back negative, my leg from the groin down was nonetheless confined to a heavy and burdensome medieval brace known as a "Thomas's splint." All my athletic dreams of one day playing rugby for England flew out the window the instant that brace went on.

I was confined for ten months in that hillside sanatorium, tied to a bed in that medieval torture device invented by the maniacal Mr. Thomas, one which caused infections just by its confining nature. My school career was ruined, I'd be given two pointless operations (one left my knee disfigured for life), injections every few hours, and I was still no further along the road to finding out what was actually wrong with me.

So the doctors turned me loose, but only if I agreed to wear a leg caliper, which was a heavy but mobile version of Thomas's splint. Once again, the caliper went from my groin down to my ankle. But I had quite a surprise when I tried to get into my trousers. While I had been five feet, nine inches tall when I'd been admitted into the hospital, I was now a bean pole at six foot three.

I had to wear the caliper all the time, even when sleeping. I limped wherever I went, for two more years. When I was finally given permission to take it off, I began exercises to strengthen my leg muscles. Swimming was the choice. I was on my way home from the community pool when I saw a magazine in a shop's window, with a bodybuilder on the cover. At that moment I became utterly determined to work hard on building back my health and athletic ability.

That was in 1951. By 1960, now grown to six feet seven and weighing in at 250 pounds, I was a contender for Mr. Universe. By 1962, I was the British Heavyweight Weightlifting Champion, and would be for three years running. The TB ward and a life confined to a leg brace were far behind me. But it was good training for the heavy costume and mask that would years later turn me into Darth Vader, villain of the universe.

When I feel a bit down from time to time—we call it "the blues"—all I have to do is think back to when I was lying in that TB ward, my future dashed, or so I believed. I remember the smile my mother always had when she visited, although she was taking in boarders back home to make ends meet.

This visit to the "dark side" of my life is the quickest cure for the blues.

It works like a charm every time!

David Prowse is a world-renowned weightlifter and bodybuilder. It is his role as Darth Vader, in George Lucas's first three *Star Wars* films (all five *Star Wars* films are ranked in the top twenty-five all-time highest-grossing movies), that has turned him into a worldwide icon among his legions of loyal fans.

22 Rolling Over the Blues

PAT SCHROEDER

When people are knocked off course it seems there are two kinds of folks. While there are obviously the hand wringers, others roll up their sleeves and plow ahead. We should all aspire to be one of the rollers and plowers!

That's the only way one ever gets out of a hole!

Former Colorado congresswoman Patricia Schroeder is president and chief executive officer of the Association of American Publishers (AAP), the national trade organization of the U.S. book publishing industry. Congresswoman Schroeder left office undefeated in 1996 after serving in the House of Representatives for twenty-four years.

23 Laughter and the Blues

BURT REYNOLDS

I've found that as an artist (if I can put myself in the category of artist), the blues sometimes come in very handy when working. I'm sure any writer can appreciate that, or any interpreter of the blues can understand it. The trick is how to chase the spiders out of your head.

For me, it's the sight of a newborn colt playing in a field, seeing things like a butterfly for the first time. And there's nothing like playing with a newborn puppy of any breed. And as shocking as it may seem, hand me a crying baby and if I can make it laugh, I'm a happy, happy man. These things of course are not always available. So I'm sure that's why I've been accused of having the same gang of people as near to me as possible for the last forty-five years when I'm working.

Dom DeLuise can ALWAYS make me laugh. As can Charles Nelson Reilly. Charles Durning always works. And I found two new ones: Adam Sandler and Chris Rock. I'm not moving up in class, they're just getting younger. And I can't forget Goldie Hawn. What a lucky son of a bitch Kurt Russell is.

In other words: laughter. I'm convinced that if we can do it all the time for at least, say, a half hour out of every hour of the day, it would work much better than vitamins, working out, and any or all uppers (not that I would know). Stay strong!

Oscar nominee and Golden Globe–winner Burt Reynolds is one of the world's best-recognized, most-beloved superstars who enjoys a professional reputation as a subtle, polished actor and director. His successes have been recognized by his receiving the People's Choice Award for Favorite All-Around Motion Picture Actor for a record six consecutive years, as well as being named the Most Popular Star for five years running and receiving the Star of the Year and Number One Box Office Star awards for five years in a row from the National Association of Theatre Owners, an unmatched record. You can visit his website at www.burtreynolds.com.

24 Blues of the Heart

DANIEL WOLFF

I wrote this poem twenty-five years ago, and yet it remains the way I approach the blues.

The Universal Joint

Whose heart hasn't been broken?
Or, set free. Maybe that's it.
Worked in a way it was never intended,
and then working that way forever.
At the moment of failure—when the senses falter—
there's a sound inside the chest as if
something was turning over and over.
But maybe it isn't broken
Maybe we're meant to reach some limit—
to freeze up tight—and then to grind past it—
so the pressure pours in, and the heart pivots,
and we move in this strange new circle
that links us up with the world.

Daniel Wolff's bestselling biography of Sam Cooke, *You Send Me*, won the Ralph J. Gleason Award for best music book of 1995. His writing on photography includes the first nationally published article on Ernest C. Withers in *Double Take*. His poetry has appeared in numerous journals, including *The Paris Review* and *Partisan Review*.

25 The Good Medicine Blues

GEORGE STEVENS JR.

When I feel a little bit down—that's my characterization of what is called the blues—I try to change the subject. There are so many prospective delights in life that I just want to cross over to the next phase.

Changing the subject? Well, how about sitting on the sofa with a springer spaniel on either side, responding to their cravings for affection.

Or turning one's attention to a challenging, creative project—maybe just moving it an inch or two down the road, but gaining tiny satisfactions by the process of making "order out of chaos."

Or, surefire relief, go to the golf course and walk nine holes alone in the afternoon air—stimulating yourself with those little challenges of "self-improvement" that make the game addictive for some of us. (And, by the way, this is often the place where one's enterprising subconscious decides to reveal the solution to the creative challenge of the day.)

Or, perhaps best of all, track down an offspring on the telephone—or these days a grand-offspring—and realize that it is in their lives that the future lies, and those lives would not be having their journey were it not for you.

That's it: pets, creativity, sport, nature, and children. There's lots of good medicine there.

George Stevens Jr. is a writer, producer, director, and founder of the American Film Institute. He has received eleven Emmys for his television work, which includes *Separate but Equal*, starring Sidney Poitier and Burt Lancaster, *The Murder of Mary Phagan*, starring Jack Lemmon, and two annual television traditions that he created, the Kennedy Center Honors and the American Film Institute Life Achievement Award. His production of *The Thin Red Line* received seven Oscar nominations, including Best Picture.

26 The Positive Side of the Blues

GENE PITNEY

The older I get, the less I get down in the dumps. I think at one time I used to, but as with other things that get better with age, I learned to accept what happens and look at the upside of the situation. Positive thinking is a wonderful tool and it can blow away the rain on any given day!

I like to work, be it mental, as in writing a song, or physical, as in cutting the grass. I can find happiness in either one and be just as satisfied when I am finished with my chore. I have been blessed with my health, a decent slice of talent, a wonderful family, and a long and continuing career. So why would I get down to start with?

Look at what you have and get on with it.

Life is great.

Enjoy it!

Rock and Roll Hall-of-Famer Gene Pitney has been making hits from the 1950s through the 1990s. Among his career singles are "It Hurts to Be in Love," "Town Without Pity," "The Man Who Shot Liberty Valence," and "(I Wanna) Love My Life Away." Artists who had hits performing his works include Roy Orbison, Bobby Vee, Rick Nelson, and the Crystals. You can visit his website at www.gene_pitney.com.

27 Quinnie's Blues

DINAH JOHNSON

Quinnie Blue was the great-grandmother whose name is the title of my most popular children's book. But that book doesn't begin to tell the tale. Quinnie Blue was a woman who, truly, was well acquainted with the blues. Here's the heart of her story:

Quinnie Blue, fast and free with her affections, was dead. No surprise to anyone that the cause of death was "sin-sickness." Married four times, unusual for her day, Quinnie was nobody's Christian woman. But her loving family laid her out, elegant, on the cooling board. And the ceremonies of death proceeded. But all the time, Quinnie was bargaining hard with her God, a good god, for her life. She promised to be a caretaker, a custodian of life, if only he would give her back her own. And God obliged. Quinnie Blue breathed anew and got on with living.

Everybody near and far, black and white, knew that even the littlest baby, the fragile one most in danger, would make it into this world all right if Miss Quinnie was the midwife.

A lifetime later, when she went home to her maker, Quinnie Blue had lived right and, don't you know, she died right.

I know the blues are real, and I should give them due respect. But it's a luxury for me to wallow in the blues. Best to have a little talk with God, commune with the spirit of Quinnie, bury the blues. So that's what I do.

And I get on with living this life.

Dr. Dianne "Dinah" Johnson is a professor of English at the University of South Carolina and the author of four books: *All Around Town: The Photographs of Richard Samuel Roberts*, *Sunday Week*, *Quinnie Blue*, and *Sitting Pretty: A Celebration of Black Dolls*. She has also written and/or edited several scholarly books. You can visit her website at www.dinahjohnson.com.

28 The One-Time Blues

RITA COOLIDGE

You only have to have the blues one time.

You don't have to stay there.

You just have to have the experience, and then you can sing about it.

Two-time Grammy Award-winner Rita Coolidge signed with A&M Records in 1971 and released a dozen albums over the next decade. Among them was the 1978 multiplatinum disc *Anytime, Anywhere*, which featured three of her biggest singles, "Higher and Higher," "The Way You Do the Things You Do," and "We're All Alone." You can visit her website at www.ritacoolidge.com.

29 Shane Beats the Blues

TIM SANDLIN

Kurt Vonnegut says a person must be depressed to write a novel, which is probably true. However, when I am depressed I have a tendency to sit on the couch and stare at that four-inch gap between my feet for several days, until the spiritual catatonia grows boring and I get up.

Boredom is the cure for long-term depression, and anything that alleviates boredom short-term—alcohol, sex with people you don't like, rage—only puts off the cure. So, after a few days of sitting there like an African violet in need of sunlight, I get up and fix a pot of Kenya AA coffee. Then I pop *Shane* into the VCR. It's a scientific fact that a person cannot remain in the dumps throughout a full viewing of *Shane*.

Alan Ladd. Jean Arthur. Jack Palance.

"Shane! Come back! Mother wants you!"

The movie will renew your faith in the inevitability of good's victory over evil, the dignity of beauty, and the inspiration brought on by a nice view.

After *Shane*, and a couple of cups of strong Kenya AA, I can return to my work, refreshed and ready to produce.

Tim Sandlin is a novelist and screenwriter who lives in Jackson Hole, Wyoming. His novels include *Social Blunders*, *Sorrow Floats*, *Sex and Sunsets*, *Skipped Parts*, and *Honey, Don't*. He also wrote the screenplays for *Skipped Parts* (starring Drew Barrymore and Jennifer Jason Leigh) and *Floating Away* (starring Rosanna Arquette, Judge Reinhold, and Paul Hogan). Sandlin runs the yearly Writers Conference in Jackson Hole.

30 Friends Can Beat the Blues

DR. MICHAEL OBENSKI

Whenever I'm feeling low, I just sit down on the floor right next to my big old golden retriever, Howdy. I try to explain what has me feeling blue, and Howdy understands. Howdy always understands. Somehow, that makes me feel better every time.

Sometimes, Howdy and I walk down to the barn and include Jake in the conversation. Jake listens carefully while quietly pounding one of his big hooves into the turf. Howdy and I know that he doesn't really understand the problem, though. We just include the old horse in our conversations once in a while because we don't want him to feel left out.

Dr. Michael Obenski owns the Allentown Clinic for Cats in Allentown, Pennsylvania, and writes a humorous column each month for *DVM* magazine.

31 Beating the Blues Daily

GARTH BROOKS

I am the youngest of six children, the baby of the family who readily admits to being a mama's boy. My mother, Colleen Brooks, was a singer in her youth, before she left the road to raise her family. She was my inspiration and my touchstone. I've often said that when I sang, I sang for her. She died in August 1999.

In addition to losing Mother, my marriage was in trouble. For two years I lived in a funk. Something very dark was growing inside me, and I couldn't seem to stop it. You might think that a good way for an entertainer to pull himself out of a down time would be to go on tour, letting nightly applause lift you up. But in so many ways, that would put you on the run from the blues. So I did the exact opposite. I decided I had been standing on the midway for too long, and went home.

For me to pull out of that dark place, I had to get out of the spotlight, put my career on hold, and move to my native Oklahoma. Once there, I had to learn to find myself as a person separate from the entertainer that had previously seemed to define me. I started to understand that I had been so passionate about my music, my career, that I never knew what day it was, let alone the hour. I was passionate about the moment, always trying to go new places. But I didn't have a clue about what was going on in the world in general, and sometimes not even in my own world. Somebody would ask me if I'd heard about this or that event, and I'd have to admit I hadn't.

That changed. I watched the television news each night, and started paying attention to my surroundings. For the first time in years I was involved in my children's lives on a day-to-day basis. For the first time in years, I was involved in the *world* on a day-to-day basis. I was a participant, and a *passionate* participant.

What I learned is that you can be passionate about many, many things. Obviously I'm passionate about my kids—but I've even become passionate about learning to cook, learning to take care of myself on very basic levels.

Over a period of time, I came to terms with so much. And I'm happier than I've ever been. I love being the father my daughters deserve, or at least trying to be that father. I love knowing about their schedules, about what they're studying, learning. I love not being the center of things—but being one who's watching others in the spotlight. And in the end, what I know is this: When the blues are coming up fast behind you, sometimes it's better to confront them quietly, alone, from a rocking chair on your own front porch.

Garth Brooks is the fastest-selling solo artist in music history. He was named Artist of the 1990s at the 1997 Blockbuster Entertainment Awards, and Artist of the Decade by both the American Music Awards in 2000 and the Academy of Country Music in 1999. The Garth Brooks Teammates for Kids Foundation can be contacted at www.touchemall.org.

32 The Cinematic Blues

DAN LAURIA

I fight the blues by watching old movies.

The costar of the hit television show *The Wonder Years*, actor/writer/director Dan Lauria has appeared in *JAG, Seventh Heaven, Law & Order, Law & Order: Special Victims Unit, Ed, Smallville, Against All Odds, NYPD Blue, Three Days In November,* and *The Fugitive,* among many.

33 How Farmers Beat the Blues

DAVE STAPLETON

I think beating the blues is the most important thing we face on a day-to-day basis. It's so damned easy to get down. In high school and college, a lost football game hit me worse than a defensive tackle ever could. But when I turned sixty this year, I was a mess for almost a week.

Now I know that lost relationships are far worse than lost ball games and aggravating birthdays. I remember the day I went to court to get my divorce. I walked out feeling like a weight had been lifted off my shoulders. But reality soon set in, and by the time I got back to my empty farmhouse, I felt like I had just flunked Life. I was standing at the front door, wondering if I could bear to go inside, when my mother and stepfather drove down the lane in their pickup.

"Dave, you wanna drive to town for dinner?" my stepfather asked.

I didn't want to bring my mother down, so I "cowboyed up," as I call it. By the time the waitress brought dessert, I'd snapped back. How could I not? I had a strong and loving family that had just ridden to my rescue. They'd be there if I needed them. But I still had to work hard at seeing the glass as half-full, and not half-empty.

Aside from that brush with "divorce blues," nothing pains me as much as hearing that a family has lost their farm. We lost ours when my father was still alive, and I know it broke his heart, as it did all our hearts. Later, I started selling insurance around rural Kansas. I finally quit because I couldn't stand to see all those good people worried sick that the land they'd had for generations was in danger of being sold at auction, and winding up in the hands of some conglomerate.

Still, I ended up a farmer, and so did my son. We're both doing all right, but we know that it's a gamble, and that it will always be a struggle. So I'd just say this: Every morning that I pick up a local newspaper and *don't* see an announcement of a forced farm auction, I beat the blues for one more day.

And maybe that's all a person can ask for!

Dave Stapleton is a farmer from Plains, Kansas.

34 The Insignificant Blues

JOAN JETT

Many things can set off a bout with the blues, and I have two ways to beat them.

The first is playing with my cats, whose unconditional love always reaches the deep place in my heart where contentment lives.

The second is walking or riding my bike by the ocean or in the woods. The power and majesty of nature calms me, centers me, and uplifts me spiritually to where anything that has bothered me begins to seem insignificant, giving me a feeling of gratefulness and serenity.

While still in her early teens, Joan Jett founded the seminal all-girl rock group the Runaways, whose hits, such as "Cherry Bomb," made them an international sensation. Her next group, Joan Jett and the Blackhearts, became a staple in the Top 10 charts and claims the number twenty-eight song of all time, "I Love Rock 'n' Roll." In 1989, Joan Jett and the Blackhearts were nominated for a Best Rock Performance by a Group Grammy Award for "I Hate Myself for Loving You." You can visit her website at www.joanjett.com.

35 The Blues and the Fiddle

DOUG KERSHAW

I didn't have the best childhood, out there in the swamps of Louisiana. We were so poor I didn't own a pair of shoes, nor did I *want* a pair, until my father committed suicide when I was seven years old and we had to move to town. I was so used to the houseboat rocking beneath me at night, like a big old cradle, that it was a long time before I adjusted to sleeping in a regular bed.

I also had to take my fiddle and go out onto the streets, wearing those tight new shoes and hoping people would pay me a dime to play them a song. If they did, I'd shine their shoes for them when the song was over. I found a great spot in front of a busy café owned by a Mr. Thibodeaux, and I set up shop with my shoeshine box. It wasn't easy, but I not only learned how to work the crowd at that young age, I also fed a family of five, Mama Rita and my three brothers. But it wasn't a Norman Rockwell upbringing and the blues knows this. It knows where it can hit you hard. The trick is not to let it. Or at least to hit *back,* hard.

When I feel sadness come upon me, and it still does at times when I'm not paying attention, I'll take my fiddle out and close my eyes. Then, I just go back into my mind and let the music flow. I think of Mama Rita playing her guitar and singing "Jolie Blon." Or Daddy Jack steering the "going-out" boat with his feet so he could save his hands to play the accordion, those nights when he'd be bringing us back up the dark bayou from another houseboat dance.

When I do this, when I slip back in time to recapture those good, if fleeting, childhood moments, the sounds and colors of all those *fais do-dos,* I feel like—how should I say it?—*light.* Yeah, that's it. I feel LIGHT. My mind drifts upward, almost leaving my physical body behind. For a second there, it's as if I've never been judged, or criticized, or hurt. It's as if I could never do anything wrong. I feel love, is what I feel. Then it's over, and I'm gone from that old time and place. I'm back in the "now" time.

I don't dwell on the past, I just plug into it from time to time out of respect for those loved ones who are now gone. And I think that's the secret. If I were to linger, the blues would hit me like a truck doing ninety miles an hour.

So, my advice is this: Learn to play the damn fiddle!

Considered to be the first Cajun superstar, Doug Kershaw and his band tour the world, appearing at major music festivals such as the New Orleans Jazz Festival. He currently performs in Branson, Missouri. You can visit his website at www.dougkershaw.com.

36 The Jurassic Blues

TOM RYMOUR

Although I'm originally from Scotland, I'm an African now, after forty-two years. I currently live and write in Johannesburg. Twice in my life, in 1952 and in 1976, I have quit a place I didn't mind leaving (Scotland and Rhodesia) to go and live among people I couldn't identify with. Will I die in South Africa? I always say that when I'm old enough to die, I shall go back to Zimbabwe. The blues will likely travel with me.

How do I currently beat the blues?

I go to the James Kitching Gallery at the University of the Witwatersrand and contemplate the tiny bones of the Jurassic mammal Megazostrodon, reminding myself that in two hundred million years, I, too, will be a fossil. Then I hit the Radium Beer Hall and nail a bottle of Tassenberg red while listening to live jazz.

Tom Rymour (who also writes as Tom Learmont) is a magazine editor, feature journalist, scriptwriter, English lipsynch/TV drama translator, and columnist, with a nonfiction publishing history in travel and bicycling.

37 The Jack Daniel's Blues

PAUL SYLBERT

Once, in Greenville, Mississippi, I lived a week of Mondays working on my second film as the co–art director. It was called *Baby Doll,* now remembered, if at all, for a thumb-sucking nymph in an overwrought-iron crib. I had arrived totally unprepared for southern winter weather, despite the experience of basic training in South Carolina ten years earlier. I had only a thin macintosh and Brooks Brothers brogans to protect me from the morning frosts, the fragile blue layer of ice in the wheelbarrows, the whistling chill off the not-too-distant river at Benoit. It was only my second feature and my first location trip. But it was a major motion picture.

To sweat in winter is to risk freezing, so I tried to stay loose. To do so, one must focus, empty the mind of all extraneous matter—in a word, flow. The question was, how does a beer drinker warm up, how does he rise like mercury to the occasion? Beer is heavy water, it sinks, it takes a sea of it to elevate. All around me at the end of the day the world toasted itself and sent eighty-proof waves blushing through its veins, while I, even in my twenties, had no hard liquor to call my own. Scotch was out. My father drank it and the odor sickened me.

Gin had been my mother's milk in Korea, but it was a default drink; there was nothing else except *sake,* not readily available in the Delta. Wine, I thought, was for ladies or dinner. At the happy hour I was not happy.

I should have known something of real significance was going to happen when a god intervened one day at lunch in the form of William Faulkner. Jockey-size, silver-haired, wedge-faced, squirelike, dandily mustached, bright-eyed, soft-spoken, tweedy, smelling of good tobacco with just a hint of something heady and alcoholic. Then and now, I thought him the best novelist living and one of the best ever. His rhythms intoxicated. That should have been a hint. And there he was, the American master of my native tongue, sitting opposite me at Doe's Eat Place in the black section of Greenville, Mississippi.

We had entered the kitchen, where white folks were permitted to eat, and were seated at a long table covered with a checked cloth surrounded by blackened woodstoves and the tantalizing smell of simmering greens and seared meat. In attendance were Elia Kazan, the film's director; Tennessee Williams, the screenwriter; Boris Kaufmann, the cinematographer; my twin brother Richard, the other art director; Faulkner's boyhood friend Ben Wasson; Chuck Bailey, the key scenic artist; and a few others I no longer remember, maybe ten people in all. Faulkner sat in Christ's seat, the approximate middle of the board. I think of it now as a First Supper.

Kaufmann, a European refugee, famous as the camera-man who worked with Jean Vigo, wanted to talk about literature. Faulkner wanted to talk about ducks. Kazan turned the talk toward politics and announced that the real problem in the South was the fear whites had of black sexual prowess. Faulkner disagreed. He said it was economic and then, in order to ward off any further attempts at serious conversation, he told a joke.

It was an earthy joke, bawdy in nature, and I won't repeat it here. But it brought a great laugh from around the table, and with it the aura of art and idolatry with which the audience had surrounded Faulkner vanished. And I, at the end of a bad week of worry, felt redeemed. He was just a man who laughed at his own jokes, lit his pipe, and smiled politely when the waiter arrived. In his honor, I lit my pipe with my trusty Zippo. He looked at me in a most kindly way and said, "Son, how can you do that? That stinks," referring to the smell of the contaminating lighter fluid. No doubt about it, he was a purist. A matchstick man. He would write you a novel for a barrel of whiskey and a can of good tobacco, provided it was unadulterated, and was not ashamed to admit it.

And that's when I received a gift from Jack Daniel, long dead, but watching from his perch on the oaken barrels above. At just that moment, the waiter asked if I'd like a drink. Forgetting that it was a dry county and thinking he meant something hard, I hesitated. The famous Nobel novelist, adept at searching men's souls, must have seen something in that hesitation and caught my eye and held it in his pale blue sight. He was questioning me, silently. I was sure of it. In what must have been a plaintive voice, I involuntarily confessed that I did not have a drink I liked, not a hard liquor, anyway. Nothing to warm the blood and whet the appetite. I was a beer baby. The waiter suggested a Coke, I nodded, and he left. Faulkner smiled, reached into his breast pocket, and took out a bottle of Jack Daniel's. No fancy silver flask, just a store-bought pint, which he unscrewed and moved toward the lip of an empty water glass in front of me.

"Why don't you try this?" he asked. I nodded and he poured. I lifted it, sniffed it, sipped it. It must have been warmed by his heart. It was nectar out of a keg. I was saved! Gods work in many ways, we know, and epiphanies come in many forms—in this case, the sweet heat of corn spirits.

Almost a half century later, I have been forced by my body's reluctance to live forever to give up hard liquor, booze, specifically that same sour mash whiskey still produced in the hills of Tennessee by the heirs of Jack Daniel. Some habits die hard. At around five o'clock every day, I experience a quick visit from the blues. Within my parched soul a flatted fifth sounds and sinks. From the bottom of the well I hear Chippie Hill singing "Trouble in Mind." Some men, under such enforced alterations of habit, have fallen into a depression. I get blue. It is not the first time. It will not be the last. I will confess that I miss the sweet solace of sour mash, but just thinking about it, sipped straight, or on the rocks on sultry days, turns it into a chaser of blue moods. The great novelist died of it. I live on, a little diminished, perhaps, without it, but hearing Chippie Hill in my head at the sinking of the day ain't all that bad.

Paul Sylbert won an Oscar for his work as production designer on *Heaven Can Wait*. The titles of his many films include *Kramer vs. Kramer*, *One Flew Over the Cuckoo's Nest*, *The Pope of Greenwich Village*, *Gorky Park*, *The Prince of Tides*, *Biloxi Blues*, *Rosewood*, *Free Willy 2*, *Sliver*, *Blow Out*, *Conspiracy Theory*, and *Wolfen*. He directed Richard Benjamin in *The Steagle* and is the author of the book *Final Cut: The Making and Breaking of a Film*, and the screenplay *Night Hawks*, starring Sylvester Stallone.

38 The Warm Weather Blues

"WEIRD AL" YANKOVIC

For me, nothing beats the blues like pouring cool chocolate pudding in my underwear on a hot summer's day.

Al Yankovic, the ultimate pop culture satirist, has appeared in his own TV specials for MTV, Showtime, and the Disney Channel and has starred in his own network series, *The Weird Al Show*, on CBS. He has won three Grammys and received an MTV Video Music Award nomination for "Smells Like Nirvana." You can visit his website at www.weirdal.com.

39 Swinging Away the Blues

JEAN ATWOOD

I don't want to sound like a travel brochure, but it's hard to get the blues in Colorado! Living in Boulder, at the edge of the Rocky Mountains, is a constant reminder that we are part of something huge and wonderful in this world.

One thing I have learned over time, though, is that we must be honest with ourselves about feelings. For years I never admitted to having a bout with the blues. Now I find it's far better to look the blues right in the eye and do something about them.

So, these days when I feel DOWN, I go UP, in a swing, that is. Maybe it's a throwback to when I was a small child with few worries. Who knows, and who cares? When I'm feeling the blues, I sometimes stop by an empty playground and swing the blues away. What's better is that I can now freely admit this!

Jean Atwood owns The Atwood Company, events-planning specialists in Boulder, Colorado. You can visit the website at www.atwoodcompany.com.

40 The High Altitude Blues

ANDREW STEVENSON

Years ago, when I was still a student, I would hum a favorite tune when I got the blues. But after being asked, in too many school choirs, to mouth the words silently because I sing so hopelessly out of tune, I soon became inhibited about my singing. Who wouldn't? So nowadays when I get the blues, I go for long walks, often in the Himalayas. The last seventeen years I've returned almost every year.

As a writer, I have the time to walk for days, maybe even a month or two, with my worldly possessions stuffed on my back, as if I were a turtle waddling under its protective shell. I set no targets and have no schedule. I hike for hours, plodding instinctively along trails through glittering irrigation channels and iridescent green paddy fields. The creaking of my backpack, the pad of my footsteps, my breathing, soon become familiar sounds.

A blast of cold wind down the valley inevitably stirs my expectations and drives me forward, but strangely there is no immediate objective, just a vague sense of going higher, into the Himalayas. I climb up steep paths in places built into rock walls or hand-carved under rock overhangs. The gentle slopes of hillsides give way to steep-sided mountains. The valleys become tighter, narrow gorges, with little direct sunlight as the landscape changes. Scarcer villages, fewer rice fields. Terraces are planted with maize and barley.

Insignificant, I weave my way through the cloud-congealed mountains to reach the arid brown Tibetan Plateau, where the light is intense. The clouds have gone and the sky is clear in the crisp morning light. The mountain summits seem so close and yet so high, and rise so precipitously. The freshness of the day at these high altitudes is all-pervasive, as if I have been reborn.

I listen to the sounds of the river snaking far below, its roar now only a dull rumble. Above, hundreds of prayer flags reach up from bamboo poles on rooftops, fluttering in the breeze. The pad of my footsteps on the ground becomes a hypnotic refrain, echoing the beat of my heart. For the time being, there are no cell phones or e-mails to distract me from what I am doing. There are no man-made machines or structures to give a sense of self-importance. We are merely ants, crawling on the surface and wrinkles and folds of this earth, itself only a tiny fragment of the universe.

The immensity of the mountains is humbling. There is an inherent spirituality about them. Perhaps it is the elevation, the blue untarnished sky, the silence, the comfortable warmth of the sun. Perhaps it is simply because so high up we are just that much closer to the gods.

Light is everywhere, reflecting off the mica in the rocks, the leaves, the river, and the snow. It seems to enter my soul, brightening the darkest corners of my heart and mind. I have an overwhelming sense of peace. I am exactly where I want to be. In the rarefied atmosphere of the Himalayas, anything seems possible. Each day's success is of my own making. I can make out of my life what I want, shaping my own destiny, casting aside expectations. I am living for the moment.

Certain there is no one there who can hear me, I sing aloud the words of a favorite song. Cautiously at first, then with increasing confidence and volume, until I can hear the echo of my voice bouncing off valley walls, reconfirming my existence. Finally, I belt out the song as loud as I can, with all my being, forcing musty air out of my lungs, and stale complacency out of my being.

I am singing. And I think it sounds great.

That's how I get rid of the blues.

Andrew Stevenson was born in Canada, but spent his childhood in Hong Kong, India, Kenya, Scotland, Malaysia, and Singapore. He now lives in Bermuda with his wife and daughter. Visit him at www.awstevenson.com.

41 The Duet Blues

CHAD & JEREMY

CHAD STUART: My recipe for beating the blues? Well, a gin and tonic works wonders. Actually it's not that simple. The drink has to be at the end of the day, and it has to be in the garden overlooking the fishpond, with the water bubbling over the rocks and the sighing of the wind in the willow tree. This definitely puts me in a peaceful frame of mind. No matter what crisis may be threatening to upset my apple cart, this is how I remind myself that it's probably not the end of the world, and that life goes on. We all need a quiet place, somewhere to retreat when things get crazy.

JEREMY CLYDE: Actors, when they meet, tend not to bother with the usual pleasantries. Instead, the question invariably is, "Are you working?" They all know (sad creatures that they are) that to be unemployed is to *have the blues*. And, equally, that to have a job probably means that utter depression and misery are being avoided, at least for the moment. Noel Coward used to say, "Work is more fun than fun," by which, of course, he meant creative work, not the night shift at the auto plant.

So . . . anything creative seems to be the answer. Write a song, paint a picture, do a dance.

Failing that, help those less fortunate than yourself.

An integral part of the British Invasion, Chad Stuart and Jeremy Clyde (Chad & Jeremy) were known for their quintessential harmonies on such hits as "A Summer Song," "If I Loved You," "Willow Weep for Me," and "Before and After." Pursuing careers from writing children's books to acting, they have recently reunited. You can visit their website at www.chadandjeremy.net.

42 Hugging Away the Blues

GRETCHEN WILSON

Sometimes my schedule can keep me on the road for a while. The hardest thing for me is being away from my daughter. When I'm missing her, I just keep reminding myself that in a few days, I'll be with her on the couch, cuddled up, and her hugs and tickles will make me forget I ever even had the blues!

Gretchen Wilson's debut single, "Redneck Woman," became one of the biggest debut singles in country history. Fueled by the phenomenal success of "Redneck Woman," her CD, *Here for the Party*, debuted at number one on the *Billboard* country chart and went platinum in four weeks.

43 When Friendly Angels Get the Blues

TERRI DERINGTON

I do get the blues sometimes. I'm from Hillsboro, which is the seat of Hill County, about forty-five minutes south of Dallas. Hillsboro has about eight thousand people and is known as "the friendliest town in Texas." I've lived here most of my life, went to school here, and graduated in 2002. Now I'm going to Hill College, with future plans to study radiology. I just got a new car and I have my own apartment, so I hold down two jobs.

One job is waitressing, six days a week at Friendly Angels Café, which is co-owned by my mother, Teresa Porter, and her partner, Deana Youngblood. I get to the café at 6:30 A.M. and leave at 3:00 P.M. I've been waiting tables for four years now, so my feet are used to the job. We're not situated close enough to the interstate for a lot of passing travelers to stop. Mostly, we get locals as customers, a variety of townspeople we've known for years.

My afternoon job is in the infant room at Rebecca's Country Day Care, taking care of the babies, which I do until 6:00 P.M. I probably don't need this second job, but I enjoy it. Right now, I've got eight babies in my care. I really love being with them, even though I'm usually tired by the time I get to the day care. But playing with the babies isn't a chore at all. It lifts me up, gives me new energy. It's hard to have the blues when you're around babies.

Hopefully, one day I'll meet the right man and settle down and raise a family of my own. I don't think Hillsboro is where I'll stay for the rest of my life. I think I might move to Colorado if I can get enough money together, and then find a place to live out there. I'm a bit tired of this Texas heat. I know that even in the summer it stays cool in Colorado. And then I'd love those snowy winters. If I moved, I'd have to leave all my friends behind in Texas, but I've always liked meeting new people.

When I feel the blues, I surround myself with the people I love, who are closest to me. Sometimes, I go home where I can be by myself. I turn on the radio, light some candles, and then just relax until the blues pass. But if I get the blues while I'm still at the café, my remedy is fast and sweet. We have some of the best homemade pies in town—ask anyone—chocolate meringue and coconut, made by either my mom or Deana. A good piece of chocolate meringue pie has been known to beat my blues on many an occasion.

Terri Derington lives in Hillsboro, Texas. You can visit the Friendly Angels Café website at www.friendlyangelscafe.com.

44 Around the Farm Blues

GEORGE JONES

I like to do a couple of things to get past the blues.

I like driving around the countryside in my car. Driving has always relaxed me, and I can listen to CDs or my satellite radio and get some great country music. I'm at my happiest and most relaxed when my wife, Nancy, is riding around with me.

The other thing I like to do is mow my property. There is something very soothing about driving a tractor around and the satisfaction of seeing well-maintained grounds.

And it's very relaxing to supervise but not actually *do* other various excavations on my farm, such as putting in a new road or pasture.

I also find that certain songs or artists, such as Hank Williams or Lefty Frizzell, can relax me. But, since music is my profession, it can also make me crazy at times.

Overall, to beat the blues, I'd just as soon head for the car or a tractor!

George Jones has given country music some of its all-time greatest vocal performances. Inducted into the Country Music Hall of Fame in 1992, his hits literally define country music, including "He Stopped Loving Her Today," "The Window Up Above," "A Picture of Me Without You," "The Grand Tour," and many, many others. You can visit his website at www.georgejones.com.

45 How to Dodge the Blues

TERRY KAY

I am mostly a dodger of the blues, but when struck down, I follow a few recommendations I have fashioned for myself over years of experience. These recommendations are as follows:

When suffering from the blues, avoid the reading of poetry. It will cause you to weep either over the beauty or the assassination of language, and weeping will only deepen the color of your blues.

Never listen to music that is labeled "the blues." You will want to compare degrees of lamentation and you will always make yourself more tragic than the music you're hearing. It's the one-upmanship of the defeatist. In the same vein, do not watch reruns of *Lassie*.

Do not place telephone calls to old girl/boyfriends. They hate you and they will make you feel even more worthless than you already do, especially when you must accept the fact that they are justified in whatever put-down they're offering.

Do not put yourself in the embarrassing position of attending a meeting of the Optimist Club. They will drive you insane.

Do not drink alcohol. It will taste too good, too fast.

Do not eat meats of any kind. You will sink into pity over the slaughter that put the commodity on your table.

And do not, under any circumstance, tell your wife/husband that they would be better off without you and your whimpering ways. They may see the wisdom in it.

Here is something else I have learned—a little trick. If you want to rid yourself of the blues, find someone who needs you and spend some time with them. When you're giving, the blues can't stay clogged up inside you. It's a fact.

I could write books about it.

Terry Kay has written many critically acclaimed novels, including the now classic *To Dance with the White Dog*, which was made into a Hallmark Hall of Fame movie for CBS. You can visit his website at www.terrykay.com.

46 Planting the Blues

PHIL RICHARDSON

My first memories are of my dad telling me about our family's history and showing me the land where my ancestors lived. For generations, they built their homes, raised their families, and worked the land in the midlands of South Carolina. So I suppose it is no surprise that I, too, would turn to the land for my livelihood.

After thirty years in the landscaping business, people still ask why I do it. It's hard work. It's dirty work. And it's totally unpredictable as a means of making a living. But my answer is always the same.

I love it.

And it's the best cure I know for the blues. The feel and smell of that rich soil touches me down deep. It binds me to it, like blood. The land is a part of me, and I am a part of the land, just as certainly as my ancestors were, who now rest beneath its weight.

This soil is my past, my present, and my future. In it, I find solace I can't get behind a desk or glass-enclosed office. On down days, and particularly on Sunday afternoons, my wife and I ride its sun-dappled roads, wander under the moss-draped oaks and towering Carolina pines. I can see what I planted thirty years ago and know I've made a difference.

But so has the land. And I am in awe of it, for it takes my sweat, my labor, and nurtures what I plant, so that for years to come, I see my mark. And I feel its mark on me. That's when I know there's no time or reason for the blues. It goes on.

Phil Richardson is the descendant of six South Carolina governors. He lives and works in his beloved sandhills of South Carolina with his wife, Sandy, and their two children.

47 Country Music Beats the Blues

JERRY ORBACH

One of the things I do if I get the blues is turn on cable television and tune to the Classic Country music channel.

After hearing George Jones sing "He Stopped Loving Her Today," or Hank Williams sing "I'm So Lonesome I Could Cry," my blues don't seem so bad.

Tony Award–winner Jerry Orbach *(Promises, Promises)* has earned a reputation as the quintessential New Yorker through his work in such films as *Prince of the City* and *Crimes and Misdemeanors*, as well as for his roles in Broadway's *42nd Street* and on NBC's *Law & Order*, for which he has received three Emmy nominations. His many motion-picture credits include *Dirty Dancing, Someone to Watch Over Me*, and *F/X*.

48 Three Steps Ahead of the Blues

DONNA FARGO

If "beating the blues" could be reduced to one word, I would choose *trust*.

Trust in life.

Trust in yourself.

Trust in God.

The blues are often caused by a rejection of some kind. When that happens to me, I trust in *life* by reminding myself of the following example: I once wrote a song titled "Funny Face," and pitched it to two different artists. I was just developing my wings, so I was fragile. I found myself terribly depressed when both artists turned down the song. Thank God they did! I recorded "Funny Face" and it was my second multimillion-selling record! We don't always know what's best for us. So now, when I don't get what I want, I remind myself of the "Funny Face" lesson: Trust in the process of life.

If you think about it, I know you'll find times in your life when disappointments turned into blessings. Make a list of those times and keep them handy for easy reference. They'll serve you well during down times.

Rethinking the landscape of your life can result in a lighter shade of blue. Consider that blue place where you've found yourself an opportunity to learn a lesson. Let the detours teach you about uniqueness, strengths, and, yes, misdirection. Don't fear that blue bump in your road. Storms and rain nourish the landscape. Your tears can help you grow, too. You never know what wonder-working events are headed your way. Maybe they'll even be disguised in blue.

Trust in life.

I was a girl with very low self-esteem, so I had trouble with my second area of trust: Trust in *yourself.* In fact, that old difficulty in trusting myself prompted me to write a book of prose and poetry a few years ago, *Trust in Yourself,* published by Blue Mountain Arts, the company that carries my greeting card line. Writing about the blues is a good way to work through them. I do it often. I don't set out to write a song, or a story, or a card. I just write to clear my head and better understand my feelings. After a few days, I read what I've written and try to get a better balance to my emotions. Then I usually put the pages in the "round file." So I'd advise anyone with the blues to write, to explore those feelings with a raw honesty, without ego games.

Remember, you can throw those thoughts away, with no one else's criticism or judgment. *You* are judging *yourself.* You are being your own shrink. You know yourself better than anyone else, and it's a lot less expensive. (Obviously, I'm talking about a case of the blues, not a case of clinical depression that may require professional help.) Feeling worthy of your own trust may be a lifelong endeavor, but it's important to come to a place of acceptance.

Trust in yourself.

I was just cruising along, doing what I loved, working the road, making records, writing and singing songs, enjoying my success . . . and *bam!* In 1978 I was diagnosed with multiple sclerosis.

Talk about the blues! And talk about rejection. Only this time it wasn't about a song that didn't get recorded. My *body* was rejecting me. I was scared, believing that my life must be completely out of sync for me to have a central nervous system disease. I'd been a teacher prior to having a music career, so I knew that I needed more knowledge about my condition. I began to read, to study the spirit, the mind, and the body. I read books on nutrition and emotional issues. My studies helped me change my diet and my thinking. Making progress in those areas boosted my confidence, but I soon realized that it was not enough. I realized that I had to get to know myself spiritually. I needed to touch base with God.

And so I read the Bible and I listened to inspirational, spiritual tapes. Eventually, the teacher in me taught the student in me that I had *feared* God instead of *trusting* Him. I discovered that I had to knock on the door if I wanted Him to answer, and that's what I did. Only when I acknowledged God and my connection to Him did my life start to pull back together, to regain some order.

Trust in God.

Finally, here's my own unofficial, always changing checklist for the blues battle:

Examine your attitudes. You may feel like you want to die. But you don't. You just want things to change. Don't allow negative feelings to control you. Remember, if you don't choose your thoughts, they'll choose you.

Listen to your heart.

Count your blessings.

Don't underestimate yourself. You have a purpose here.

Love really *is* the answer. It will break down walls.

Don't entertain resentments. Forgive even when you don't feel like it. (Remember, you're doing it for *you!*)

Get close to nature. Get close enough to a butterfly to examine the intricacy of its wings. Embrace the awesome scope of nature. You'll soon realize you are a part of something big.

Getting over that mountain of blues requires more than thinking and talking. There comes a time when you actually have to climb.

Life is the most precious gift we're given. It's up to us to protect it. Like I said, trust! You never know what wonder-working things are headed your way!

Donna Fargo's 1972 debut album, *The Happiest Girl in the Whole USA,* earned her a Grammy and established her as an important country-pop crossover artist. She was the first inductee into the North American Country Music Association's International Hall of Fame. Her books, cards, and calendars are put out by Blue Mountain Arts. You can visit her website at www.donnafargo.com.

49 The Food Blues

DR. JOYCE BROTHERS

When I feel blue, which is very rare, I cook "comfort food" for myself that I remember from childhood. Tapioca or rice pudding.

There is research that shows that comfort food really does comfort.

Dr. Joyce Brothers is considered the dean of American psychologists. Her columns appear in more than 175 newspapers, reaching twenty-two million readers worldwide. She is the author of ten books.

50 The Starting Over Blues

KRISTINA COPKOV

I was born in Croatia, which was part of the former Yugoslavia. When I have the blues from time to time, I remember my father's words to me. "In every difficult situation, remember your strength and faith in God. Don't be afraid, don't feel sad, and don't look back. Just move ahead. And climb. How high doesn't matter. If you go up two steps and fall back ten, it's all right. All that matters is that you're climbing."

I was six years old when he told me this, and I never forgot it. Over the years, through many visits from the blues, his words not only helped me pull through, they are now a part of my survival skills. Growing up in a Communist country, I saw the horror of World War II. My family lived in a house we loved, surrounded by our vineyards, but a house that was destroyed in an instant by a bomb. And yet, no one in our family was hurt, so we considered ourselves lucky that day.

I married at the age of twenty-three. Three years later, I was divorced with two very young children to raise. My ex-husband went on to become a successful doctor in Belgrade, and I went on to become a single mom with no financial help. At this stage of my life I didn't cry or pity myself. I didn't have the time. I left my children with my mother in Croatia, and I moved to Milan, Italy, where I knew I could find work. I sent most of my money back home to my mother. My father had already died by this time, but I knew my mother could provide a safe place. And she did. My children were in a warm and loving home. It was hard being far away from them, but to this day they talk of how their grandmother taught them to believe in themselves.

After several years in Italy, I finally had enough money to move us to Canada. We arrived in New York first, where my brother lived. I still have a photo of the three of us that day. You can see uncertainty on our faces because starting over in a new culture and land is not easy. But you can also see determination there.

Many years later, I find myself up against the blues again. I'm sixty-six years old, an age when most people are settling down for the last part of their lives. And yet, I'm about to be divorced for the second time. So it's time to start over. The house I loved, with my garden of flowers and birds, was just sold. I've recently moved to an apartment and am adjusting to apartment living all over again, the way I did as a young woman in Milan. To beat the blues, I still think of my father's words to me, those many years ago. "Climb. How high doesn't matter." And I feel the presence of my mother. Before she left Canada for the last time, on her last visit, I kissed her good-bye at the airport. I didn't know then I would never see her again. But I think she knew. She said to me, "I will be with you always." And she is.

So, I have decided that I won't let the blues catch me. And I think one of the best ways is exercise. It's not just good for your health, but it's hard on the blues. I go out each day and I run long distances. As I do, I reflect on my past, and I think about my present. I have wonderful children and grandchildren. Maybe my apartment means that I have no backyard of flowers and birds, but many, many people in this world have no home at all, not even food to eat. That thought alone is enough to make me stop feeling the blues. Tomorrow will bring another wonderful day. And remember that love is a powerful tool, one that can always beat the blues.

Kristina Copkov lives in Toronto, Canada. She hopes one day to open a bed-and-breakfast.

51 Organizing the Blues

WYNONNA JUDD

When I have the blues I start organizing my house—if you want to get out of a funk, clean up your junk! Start with the basics, the sock and underwear drawers, and move up the stuff chain. The more clutter you remove from your physical world, the more your emotional load will lighten. As you start to feel more organized, a cleansing process begins. There is an additional benefit to organizing your drawers and closets. I usually find something in my junk that sparks a memory that will cause me to laugh or cry, a recollection that will take me to a different place.

Then I remember "this too shall pass."

Very soon the darkness turns to light and I can move on.

I also try to remember a lesson I learned from Mother Teresa's example: There are people with far greater problems than mine. That's when I say to myself: Quit complaining! Get off your butt and do something that helps ease somebody else's troubles!

As lead vocalist of the Judds, Wynonna was part of a phenomenon seldom seen in the industry. The mother/daughter duo won over sixty major industry awards, including five Grammys, nine Country Music Awards, and eight *Billboard* awards. Solo, Wynonna has won nineteen major industry awards, including the Academy of Country Music's Top Female Vocalist. You can visit her website at www.wynonna.com.

52 How to Beat the Blues in L.A.

STEPHANIE GERMAIN

Whenever those blues try to take control of my day, I just put my work down, pack my three beautiful children into the van, and we head off to the park. As a child growing up in New York City, Central Park was my playground. Sharing the experience now with my children helps chase away those demons in my head.

My new hometown, Los Angeles, has so many parks to choose from. Sometimes we go to the one with the ice-cream truck and duck pond. Sometimes my oldest child (the only one at present who can talk, since her twin brother and sister are still babbling) chooses the park she likes best, the one with the orange slides. Other times, we head to the park that's close to our favorite market so we can stop for take-out food. Then we spread a blanket on the grass and have a picnic. Just play-ing with my three children, hearing their laughter and joy at the simplest things, like a game of tag or seeing who can go higher in a swing, is the best medicine for my blues any day.

Stephanie Germain is a film producer who lives in Los Angeles. Among her many production credits are *Ike: Countdown to D-Day, The Day After Tomorrow, The Pilot's Wife, The King of the World, The Princess and the Marine,* and *Too Rich: The Secret Life of Doris Duke.*

53 The Mystery of the Blues

THOMAS PATRICK STRAW

When I sat down to write this essay an hour ago, I had a pretty strong case of the blues. I was in the midst of self-pity. Things haven't been going as well as I'd hoped lately. Most of us know *that* story. So, I finally gave up writing and wandered downstairs, away from my computer, away from the dreaded blinking cursor, to the mindless television set. I had no idea that in a few moments I would be party to a miracle.

When my wife walked into the room, she had a look on her face that was part surprise and part joy.

"What's up?" I asked her. Then, all of a sudden, I remembered the pregnancy test kit we had purchased just this morning! We have been dreaming of having a child for some time. And we have been trying harder than either of us dared to admit.

I just stared at her, waiting.

"Yes," was all she said, and all she had to say.

As I write this, it's been just a few minutes since I have received this news. My wife and I have created life, the greatest of all miracles. And from that life, I have found renewed inspiration. The blues are long gone. How could I have had them in the first place?

If you wrote this story in a script, you would be laughed out of the reading room. I went from having the blues and self-pity, to hearing the best news I could ever get. I'm going to be a father. A parent. Will the gifts at our baby shower be blue or pink? I don't know, and I don't care. That's a mystery I can live with for a few months. Now, of course, I can't tell everyone out there to have a baby if they want to beat the blues! But it sure doesn't hurt if you're deeply in love, and committed, and as ready as my wife and I are. But I can tell you this:

This is the happiest day of my life!

Thomas Straw is a webmaster and digital photographer. He and his wife, Jennifer, live in Pittsburgh. They are expecting their first child. You can visit his website at www.budandtravis.com.

54 The Creative Blues

TOMMY JAMES

When I'm left alone too long, I have a natural tendency to get moody and depressed. That's made me a good target for the blues in the past, so nowadays I try not to let that happen. I'm a Christian, so as soon as I get up in the morning, I get myself centered by reading Scripture. I pray. And so does my wife, Linda. Prayer takes me to another place. It turns my whole day around.

And then I write.

I sometimes have a cowriter, but most of the time I prefer to write alone. I don't know if the act of writing causes my brain to produce a little extra serotonin or what. I just know that writing almost instantly makes me feel good. It makes me feel whole again. I sit at my piano, or at the synthesizer, or I grab my guitar, and then I bang out whatever mood I'm in. Creativity almost always saves me from the blues.

However, if none of the above works, I just go to bed.

Tommy James's many hits songs include "Hanky Panky," "I Think We're Alone Now," "Mirage," "I Like the Way," "Gettin' Together," "Out of the Blue," "Get Out Now," "Mony Mony," "Do Something to Me," "Crimson and Clover," "Crystal Blue Persuasion," and "Sweet Cherry Wine." Tommy performs to sold-out crowds across the country and has filmed a PBS music special, *Sixties Pop Rock Reunion,* which is currently airing on PBS. You can visit his website at www.tommyjames.com.

55 The Broken-down Bus Blues

GERALD WILLIAMS

"Give the World a Smile" has been the Melody Boys Quartet theme song since 1949, when I started singing bass for the group at the ripe old age of sixteen. Back then, it was easy to give the world a smile. I was young and living my dream of singing professionally with my favorite southern gospel quartet. Riding for hundreds of miles in a cramped car, sitting in the front seat of a 1948 Chrysler DeSoto between two other guys (since our suits took up the space where I might have otherwise sat in the back) was no problem! I was just glad to be where I was, doing what I loved to do!

More than fifty years later, I'm blessed to still be anchoring the bass spot for the Melody Boys, still doing what I love to do. But getting there to do it is more of a problem for me now! I can't tell you the number of hours I've spent in a broken-down bus, waiting on a tow truck; or the number of times I've gotten us down the road by adjusting a faulty regulator with a rubber band, or wiring a fuel valve open with a coat hanger. And the hours we've spent stuck in bumper-to-bumper traffic are too many to count. Times like those make me ready to switch from southern gospel to the broken-down bus blues!

But every now and then, something happens to snap you out of it and send the blues on down the road. Recently, we were traveling west on I-20, just east of Fort Worth, Texas, when we came upon an eighteen-wheeler that had jackknifed on the rain-slick highway. Another eighteen-wheeler had run into the ditch, trying to avoid a collision with the first truck. Traffic was stopped dead for more than an hour while tow trucks and rescue units cleared the highway.

I was standing in the door well, bemoaning our situation with the driver, when I saw a nicely dressed older lady carefully picking her way through the cars and coming toward our bus. It was clear to see that she was in distress. I opened the door and asked how we could help.

"I'm so embarrassed," she said. "I've never done anything like this before! But my friends and I are desperate!" She pointed in the direction of a Cadillac Escalade, where two other ladies were climbing out and heading our way. "We absolutely have to get relief soon, or we'll be forced to show our behinds to everyone on I-20! Would it be possible for us to use your bathroom?" She was begging by this point in time.

"Of course," I told her. "Don't worry about it. Just make yourselves at home." We handed the ladies an empty, plastic Wal-Mart bag for their used bathroom tissue, explaining that they shouldn't flush anything down the pipes. Soon all three women filed down the hall of the bus, each gratefully taking a turn in our bathroom.

Later, as the ladies made their way back to their car, carrying the Wal-Mart bag, smiling, and waving good-bye, I thought about the first line from our theme song: "Give the world a smile each day, helping someone on life's way." I don't think I'll ever sing that line again without remembering those ladies and how "helping someone on life's way," no matter how minor the task, gave us a smile right back!

Gerald Williams began his gospel singing career in 1949, with the Melody Boys Quartet. He has also contributed his bass voice to several other groups, namely the Plainsmen Quartet, the Venable Quartet, and Rosie Rozelle and the Searchers. In 2000, Gerald Williams collaborated with his daughter, Judy Cox, on an autobiography, *Mighty Lot of Singin'*. You can visit his website at www.themelodyboysquartet.com.

56 Cooking Up the Blues

TY HERNDON

Cloudy, overcast days always bring out the blues in me. More often than not, I can meditate and pull myself back up out of the dumps. But when that doesn't work, I have the perfect backup plan: a family gathering.

I call up my relatives and invite them to dinner, then I go buy groceries and come home to cook. I make chicken fried steak, mashed potatoes, white gravy, biscuits and corn bread, green beans, corn on the cob, lima beans. I guess it's a three-part therapy starting in the grocery store, moving to preparing the food in the kitchen, and ending with sharing a meal and an uplifting conversation with family.

The blues fly right out the window.

Ty Herndon has had many chart-topping country hits, including "What Mattered Most," "Living in a Moment," and "It Must Be Love." Most recently, he and Tanya Tucker recorded a duet of the Elton John/Kiki Dee hit, "Don't Go Breaking My Heart." Visit his website at www.tyherndon.com.

57 The Espionage Blues

SHERRY SULLIVAN

I know the blues well. It's been a visitor since I was seven years old. Here's why. September 23, 1963. It's a glorious autumn day and I am doing second-grade arithmetic at my desk. Earlier that morning at a tiny airport outside our home of Waterbury, Connecticut, my father, Geoffrey Sullivan, was saying good-bye to my mother, Cora. He is handsome, with dark hair and striking blue eyes. Still only twenty-eight years old, he's now a private pilot with eight years of Air Force experience behind him. Later this day, he and Alexander Rorke Jr. (journalist and son of a prominent New York politician) are going on another one of their mysterious trips.

When Mother drives Daddy to the airport, he takes off his Saint Christopher medal and gives it to her. Mother thinks this is strange, for he's never done this before. She watches as the plane taxis down the runway and lifts off, my father sitting behind the controls. Daddy will be back home in five days. (I wouldn't know until many years later that the two were anti-Castroites, most likely working for the CIA.)

While my mother went to her job at the beauty shop each morning, and I got on the yellow bus and went to school, my father was switching planes, passengers, and destinations (he filed a flight plan to Panama and Nicaragua) until he was out of touch with the control towers. As I write this, it is March, in the year 2004. We have neither seen nor heard from Geoffrey Sullivan since that autumn day in 1963.

None of the desperate attempts by wives, parents, or friends could bring the two men back. As for me, I made it a point to rush home from school every day and wind Daddy's watch. I thought if I could keep it ticking, like a sure and steady heartbeat, nothing bad could happen to him, wherever he was. In many ways, I'm still winding that damn watch.

Two years after my father disappeared, my mother received a call that he'd been in a Cuban prison and was on his way home. Our family gathered and waited far into the night, only to learn from a quick telephone call that it was a horrible mistake.

Never truly able to move on with her life, even after a second marriage, my mother died last year, still beautiful and far too young, at the age of sixty-seven. And as for me? Well, this is why the blues and I joined up. My sadness over losing my father, a melancholy that seemed to eat at me internally, led me down the road of depression, even drugs, until I woke up one freezing January morning in 1984, at the age of twenty-eight, and decided that I would begin my own search for Geoffrey Sullivan, who was twenty-eight himself the last time I saw him. I have been searching ever since.

In my art gallery, there hangs a painting of Geoffrey Sullivan, done from an old photograph my mother gave me. He is still handsome, a mischievous grin on his face. You can see the daredevil in his blue eyes. My mother told me that when the two of them were courting, he would fly his airplane beneath the bridge of the small Maine town where she lived. I like to think that I inherited his sense of adventure.

I still wake in the heart of the night and yearn to know what happened to him. Some mornings, I rise and pour a cup of coffee. I turn on my computer to some new information coming in from contacts I've made: "Your father is still alive and in one of Castro's prisons. A man just released after thirty years says an American has been there since the 1960s. They call him Sully." Or, "We have it on good authority that your father and Alex crash-landed in Cuba. They were dragged from the plane and executed on the spot. Your father put up a brave fight." And so it goes, on and on.

The blues is not all my life is about, otherwise living would be folly. So to beat the blues, I just put things in a proper perspective. I pull out all the positive ammunition. For instance, I have friends I care deeply about, and I know they care about me. We laugh a lot, and laughter is a good medicine. I have a lovely daughter and two lovely grandchildren. I love cooking, I love my art gallery, I love the sunsets I often see captured in the waters of Penobscot Bay. I've learned how to juggle.

As I said, the blues is my companion, not my enemy.

Sherry Sullivan is a private detective living in Stockton Springs, Maine. She is the founder of Forgotten Families of the Cold War, a national support group. You may visit her website at www.forgottenfamilies.com.

58   The Healing Blues

JESSE COLIN YOUNG

The blues was the founding force in my music, whether it came through Elvis, Hank Williams, or my folk mentors Lightnin' Hopkins and Mississippi John Hurt. So the word *blues* was never a downer for me. It was more like a wild garden filled with the raw, sweet smell of life . . . crazy love, wanderlust, betrayal, lost friendship, emptiness, loneliness, anger, and desperation. When I picked up my first guitar at the age of fifteen, I found a place to put all these feelings that raged in me. It was the beginning of a lifelong love affair that still burns strong.

When my treasured Ridgetop house in California burned down in a wildfire in October of 1995, I was so far down that the blues looked like up to me. As soon as we arrived at our little farm in Hawaii to heal, I bought a new Mesa Boogie amp from a friend, pulled my old Les Paul off the wall, and decided it was time to learn to play slide guitar. The emptiness was so intense that only that loud, mournful sound could fill it. I began to write songs, blue songs, hard-to-sing-without-crying songs, and, strangely enough, they lifted me up and carried me out of that desolate time.

The healing power of music is so strong that sometimes when I'm singing I feel like a minister preaching the gospel of life, which for me is deeply entwined with the gospel of love. I know all of us who play and sing have touched this powerful stream, this sometimes hidden river of feelings that binds all of humanity together. What a blessing it is to do this work. I'm just gonna keep on keepin' on.

Blessed with a career that has included Top 10 hits with the Youngbloods and solo recordings consistently on the Billboard Top Albums chart, Jesse Colin Young has dedicated his life to giving back to the world he and his family live in. You can visit his website at www.jessecolinyoung.com.

59 Jade's Message for the Blues

HELEN VROON

Missing your child is a lot heavier than having the blues. But I was invited to be in this book, and that's what I want to talk about. Maybe others out there will read this and understand. Maybe something I say can help them in some small way.

My daughter Jade died in May 2002. It was very sudden. I had taken her for tests when she wasn't up to her usual self. Twice, we were told to go home, that nothing was wrong. One morning, Jade couldn't go to school. When I saw her face, I knew it was serious. The ambulance couldn't come so I got her into my van and drove her to the hospital. She died on the way, but I didn't know that at the time. The doctor finally looked in my eyes and told me the words no parent wants to hear: "We tried to revive her, but we couldn't." Her heart had enlarged to three times its size. It was over that fast. I remember how quiet the room was. There was screaming, but it was all inside my head. Jade was sixteen. Slim, pretty, a tennis player. She had just gotten the braces off her teeth a month before. My baby girl. My first dream come true. My treasure. My daughter.

The nurses let me remove all the tape and pads on Jade's chest that were connected to the machines. Gently, I took them off and I disconnected myself from reality. I held her to me, and rocked her for the last time. This was the child who was so thoughtful and kind to everyone.

I knew very little about death before that day. How do I go on without her? That's what I kept asking myself. Often, when I couldn't bear it anymore, I'd find myself out at her grave, at Pleasant Gardens Cemetery. I soon discovered I was a member of a very unusual club. I wasn't the only parent in this pain, and now I understood what others were going through.

Jade was the third student from her high school that we buried that spring. It seemed as if our small community was under attack. But I had three other children, younger than Jade, who needed me. I tried to keep up with their lives. I went to school games when I could find the strength and courage to do so. Often, another mother or father would approach me in the stands. "Are you Jade's mom?" they'd ask. When I'd nod, they would say, "I'm so-and-so's mom." Or maybe it was a dad. Another parent who had lost a child. Before long we'd be sitting there, holding hands, maybe even crying. There is strength in numbers.

But what happens when you're alone, when it's late at night and the other kids are asleep? That's what you're not prepared for. It's just you and your hurting heart. It isn't easy.

Time passed, and I lay alone at night, praying for inspiration. One such night, I decided to design a decal for my car (and for anyone else who wanted one), a small way to pay tribute to a wonderful girl named Jade. I wanted the decal to tell a story and to honor Jade all at the same time. I thought about this decal for a lot of long nights. Finally, the idea came to me. I got up out of bed and found some paper and scissors. I would make beautiful angel wings. They would represent heaven. Because I'm not an artist, I folded my paper like a child might do, and began to cut the wings. When I unfolded them, to my surprise, there was the shape of a heart cut right in the center of my wings. Then I drew a fish, the symbol for Jesus. I wrote the word *Jade* inside the fish, to show that she was now with Him. As a mother, I had to connect with her and make her smile. I asked myself, What does Jade want, what would make her happy? Then it came to me. She would want all life here on earth to believe. So, I added the word *believe* in beautiful script below the wings. I felt I had given Jade a voice. I had the decal made and gave it to friends, who gave it to friends, who gave it to friends.

Sometimes, this world spins out of control. We humans are often too busy. One morning not so long ago, my kids weren't ready for school. I had to get to my job at the restaurant where I work. We ended up late, and in a rush out the door. In the van, the twins were bickering again. My oldest son, Clayton, needed more money than I had in my purse. It started out as a blue Monday. Then we saw it. All at the same time, we shouted, "Look!" The car in front of us had a Jade decal on the back windshield. I smiled. The twins smiled. Clay smiled.

Not long ago I had one of the dreams I've had of Jade. She came bounding up onto the front porch to talk to her sister and me, and hug us. Blonde, tall, athletic. Then she turned to leave. "Jade," I said, "don't go." She turned and looked back at me, smiled that Jade smile. "Oh, Mama," she said. "Nobody stays forever."

If I can give you any message for beating the blues, for those times when you feel down and you need a lift, when you think life might not be a great idea, I'd like for it to be a message from Jade Vroon. Remember these two things. First, "You must believe," and second, "Nobody stays forever."

Helen Vroon has three children at home. She lives in Summertown, Tennessee, and can be contacted at helenvroon@hotmail.com.

60 How Horses Lick the Blues

LYNN ANDERSON

Horses have always been my cure for the blues—my golf, my tennis, my psychiatrist, though at times they might need a little help on that last one. Playing with my horses has always been soothing to my soul.

Their huge eyes sucker me in every time. They seem to be mirrors to *my* soul. Whether I'm just grooming, brushing and scratching, feeding them a carrot or an apple, or leading a pregnant mare to grass and massaging her stomach to feel that baby move . . . whether I'm playing with a new colt in the pasture, or teaching that yearling to stand tied . . . it's all good. The big plus is loping out across a field, or looking at the valley after we've climbed to a mountaintop together, or chasing cows. But it's all good.

My Gramma Grace taught me about horses. And she told me this many moons ago: "There's nothing better for the inside of a person than the outside of a horse."

I think that quote has been attributed to everyone from Socrates to Teddy Roosevelt, but for me, it was from Grace's lips to my ear.

Her country and pop hit, "Rose Garden," made Lynn Anderson an international superstar and won her a Grammy Award for Best Female Vocal Performance of the Year. She was named Female Vocalist of the Year by the Academy of Country Music and the Country Music Association, as well as *Record World*'s Female Artist of the Decade. "Rose Garden" was followed by a string of hits, including "How Can I Unlove You," "Cry," "Keep Me in Mind," "What a Man My Man Is," "Rocky Top," "Under the Boardwalk," and "Top of the World," which won CMA Song of the Year. You can visit her website at www.lynn-anderson.com.

61 Partying Away the Blues

TROY BODY

I grew up in the shadow of mountains. Harlan, Kentucky, is on the Tennessee/Virginia border and is considered as far away as Mars by my fellow Kentuckians. My grandfather came to the Appalachian Mountains, like most black men, to mine its coal. We were surrounded by hills bloated with coal that wrapped around us like loving arms, arms that protected us from the ills of city living. Oddly enough, the embrace was so tight that we were often cut off from the *benefits* of city living, as well.

In the South, you are taught to suffer in silence. Enduring makes you stronger. Keeping a stiff upper lip will get you through "it," whatever "it" is. This notion is a commonly held assumption. So don't whine. Keep it to yourself. Everything will be all right.

Not for me. I talk too much.

I like parties. I like calling my friends together, wherever and whenever I please. The entire notion of a friend is solely for selfish reasons. Friends exist for our pleasure. Therefore, if I begin to feel blue, I sweep those feelings under the carpet of friends woven together in the form of a party; then I tell them everything. I pour my heart out in seconds.

We have had dessert parties, Saturday afternoon parties, preparties (that's a party before the party), happy-to-be-alive parties, and my personal favorite: nothing-to-do-but-a-party parties. These parties are not elaborate. It's the fellowship that is most important.

You see, the blues, like all things, have a weight to them. Some issues are heavier than others, but they are all taxing just the same. Sharing your life with others, the good times and the bad, spreads the weight of the world across the shoulders of everyone in your life.

In a small town, where all the neighbors know your business, you're only kidding yourself if you don't believe they are keenly aware of your ups and downs. Your life is an open book. So let them read it. Call your friends together and tell them: "I cannot do this on my own." Open your best bottle of bourbon, the one you were saving for a special day. Play that seventies funk and soul. Laugh loudly. Curse because you're grown. Eat until you're dizzy. And be grateful your nosey-ass neighbors care enough about you to share your sad times.

Troy Body is the West Virginia commissioner of culture and history.

62 The Polka Blues Cure

STEVE POPOVICH

I think the best way to beat the blues is to play a polka. It's the People's Prozac. I grew up in the coal patch. Nemacolin, Pennsylvania, was the company town of Buckeye Coal, where my father worked. I was called a "hunky," coal mining management's derisive term for ethnics, those immigrants and "foreigners" in their employ. Don't get me wrong, I love being a hunky. I'm a Serb/Slovenian/Croat and proud of it. In fact, despite tensions between these ethnic groups in the Yugoslavia of yesterday and today, I grew up admiring and respecting other cultures. The friends of my youth were black and white, WASP, Catholic, and Jewish, and a wide mix of Serbs, Poles, Greeks, Croats, Slovenians, Italians, and Irish. So I guess it was appropriate that this mix of new Americans lived in Nemacolin, which was named after an Indian chief.

My father and his brothers played tamburitza, Yugoslavian folk music, mostly from Croatia and Serbia. So at an early age I learned to play the tambura and sing hundreds of songs in Serbo-Croatian. Even though I played in a rock 'n' roll band through high school, and went on to become a record executive initially working with rock, pop, and country acts, I never forgot my first musical love: ethnic music.

As it turned out, it was an ethnic hero, America's Polka King, Frankie Yankovic, who helped me get work at CBS Records, my first job in the music industry. Years later, while signed to my Cleveland International label, Frankie won the first Grammy Award ever given for polka. I've lost the blues many times to "Beer Barrel Polka" and "Blue Skirt Waltz."

Of all the traditions immigrants brought to America, music is one of the greatest. So if you try my remedy, the polka blues cure, remember to lift a glass and toast all the hunkies that kept this music alive and vital right into the twenty-first century.

Steve Popovich has been a music industry executive since 1972. He has worked with Johnny Cash, Bob Dylan, Bruce Springsteen, Michael Jackson, Tom Jones, and Meatloaf, among others. You can visit his website at www.clevelandintl.com.

63 The Other Side of the Blues

JUDY HENSKE

As far as the blues goes, I am of two minds, like a workbench on which there are two chain saws. The blues is what happens when the two sides of you are at war with each other. You have to get in touch with both sides of your nature with the blues, your male side and your female side. Then, after you spend some time on each side, you have a better chance of coming out on the "other" side of the blues. Which is the middle.

GETTING IN TOUCH WITH YOUR MALE SIDE

BE CAREFUL!

If you have the blues on account of a no-good man, and you're in touch with your male side and you go and find his truck and get up on the hood and kick in his windshield, he could get picky about it and you will go to jail and they'll put you in what is called "the tank," and there, you will meet a lot of other women with the blues who have only gotten in touch with the male side of their natures. I'm not exactly sure if this windshield thing is a felony, but if it is, you'll have a JURY TRIAL! If the jury is all women, they'll let you go!

GETTING IN TOUCH WITH YOUR FEMALE SIDE

This takes dollars and interior-decorating skills.

Okay, first you *must* have handy a one-hour tape of the saddest, most pitiful, pathetic, and depressing songs ever recorded. (My tape includes "Oh My Papa" by Connie Francis, "He Stopped Loving Her Today" by George Jones, and, most important, "I Fall to Pieces" by Patsy Cline and everybody else who ever recorded it, which fills out the hour.)

Next, you must get out your pictures of all your dead pets and put them where you can concentrate on them. (You'll be reminded of how much better you could have been to them, and now you'll never have the chance.) As long as the dead pets are out, it wouldn't be a bad idea to make a list of all your failures. It's a good thing to have handy.

Now, interior decoration.

You did this when you were "anticipating" the blues. You're going to convert a room in your house into a Blue Room! Cover all windows with blue scarves and blue cellophane. Get some *huge* glass bottles and put strings of blue Christmas lights in them! Put blue flowers all over in blue glass vases! A blue rug wouldn't be bad. Now you've got a blue room! Redecorating has given you a good feeling! Put on your best bra and underpants. Put on a tight black catsuit, and then a long, sheer blue caftan over it. Backless, blue satin mules with feather pom poms. Sequins? SURE! Next, lots of lipstick and eyeliner. A little rouge. Now you look like Peggy Lee! (Or, if you're real big like I am, a drag queen.) Take a blue Valium. Sit in your blue room drinking blue Curaçao from a blue goblet while you listen to your tape and do all the other stuff.

You are now in touch with your female side.

You have come out on the other side of the blues.

Singer/songwriter Judy Henske recorded six folk/rock/blues albums in the 1960s. This body of work earned her the title "Queen of the Beatniks." Rock critic Dave Marsh called Henske: "a talent so diverse in what she's good at that she's beyond all categories except *legendary* and *great*." You can visit her website at www.judyhenske.com.

64 Riding Out the Blues

NICOLE MCBREAIRTY

I spent ten years of my childhood in eight different foster homes. I lived at one home for nine days, and another for nearly four years. I don't like the story of my life and I don't like to tell it; mostly because none of it really matters anymore. What matters is that I made it.

When I was young, I sat stiff and stared at walls for hours. I'd pick a hole or crack and wish myself to fit into it, headfirst, so my eyes would find blackness and my ears would stuff with plaster. How do you know that you are sad when you're a child? I didn't. I just wanted to disappear. I hid under my bed and spoke with clumps of dust and pebbles. I floated high above myself and felt nothing, or at least what I thought was nothing.

The feeling still comes over me now and then. I know now that it's sadness. Some folks call it the blues. These days, I am strong enough to identify the sadness, to call it by its name. This can only weaken it. So I say out loud, "I think I'm sad." Sometimes I have a cry and when the cry is done, I rise up stronger than ever.

But most times, I pick up my guitar and play my favorite songs. The sad songs. The really sad songs. I suspect this is the Irish in me. I play and sing until the feeling passes over me like a cool wave. Or until the pressing of my fingers on the guitar strings reminds me again that I am alive, and that life is short, and here I am again, strong enough to ride the wave.

This is when I smile. This is my own personal victory.

Nicole McBreairty is the owner of McBreairty Paints, a small wallpaper business that she founded in southern Vermont. An aspiring poet and songwriter, her hobbies include guitar, running, and playing with her dog, Chex.

65 Dousing the Blues

BOBBY BRADDOCK

I usually beat the blues with what I call "nipping it in the bud," but actually it's called "cognitive therapy." I picked it up over twenty years ago from a book titled *Feeling Good* by Dr. Kenneth Burns. At the first sign of depression, I do a quick inventory. I ask myself, Did someone recently say something to hurt my feelings? Did I just have a negative thought? Did I just hear an old song that triggered an unpleasant memory?

As soon as I identify what it is that's trying to bring me down, I immediately do damage control and cast the culprit out. Then I go my merry way.

The blues can spread quickly—put it out right away or you could end up with a forest fire.

Nashville Songwriters Hall of Fame member Bobby Braddock is one of country music's most successful and prolific songwriters. Among his thirty-five Top 10 country singles are thirteen number one hits, including "Golden Rings," "D.I.V.O.R.C.E.," "He Stopped Loving Her Today," "Time Marches On," "Texas Tornado," and "I Wanna Talk About Me."

66 The Night Jimmy Smith Lit Up the Blues

PORTER FOX

It happened in the Hollywood Bowl, as Los Angeles epiphanies probably often do. There were twenty thousand people wrapped around the old amphitheater, a million stars overhead, my friend and his girlfriend next to me, Beverly Hills rolling to the city like ripples in a green carpet. The Clayton-Hamilton Jazz Orchestra filled the stage, and off to the side, Jimmy Smith was lighting it up on the B3 organ.

It was dark in the cheap seats, maybe the same darkness that had worked its way into my life. I'd been living in Southern California for two years, working a job that tore at my heart and pride, living in a town that made me sad almost every day. I'm from the Northeast—an island cased in granite on the Gulf of Maine, where the ocean looks like a field of diamonds under the morning sun. Where I grew up the butcher was my Little League coach and my friend's father the police chief. I felt lost in the sprawling housing tracts of Orange County, where people would as soon avoid you as say hello. But the money was good and the job offered a future, so I stayed on. And did what I could. And hated every day I lived there, until that night with Jimmy.

He was on a tear. This was in 1999 when he was healthy and his genius was at its peak. The orchestra was hot and practically drowning him out. I was thinking a million thoughts, rubbing my hand over the concrete seats, watching my friend and his girlfriend fight, thinking things you can't write a song about or even explain to anyone. Then Jimmy hit a groove in the upper octave I can only describe as perfect. The syncopation, the melody. The crowd stood and roared. We couldn't help it. Jimmy played faster. Jeff Hamilton bobbed his sax to keep the orchestra at pace. Jimmy played faster still. His torso was rigid, his hands dancing over the keys, his body seemingly possessed.

It could have been anything, but what I saw was a beam of light shooting up from behind Jimmy's back. It may have been a spotlight, but it wasn't there before the set started. It may have been a reflection, or even something to do with the three empty bottles of wine at our feet. It doesn't matter what it was, because it drew a line through the dark sky and changed my life. And here's the only way I can explain it—and the way I've explained it to dozens of friends stuck in a similar rut.

The light is your life. The orchestra is everything else. When the tune heats up, the horns kick in, the drums pick up the pace and a 747 roars overhead, look for the beam and listen. Listen hard, because there's one riff in all the confusion that's your own, and you can hear it crystal clear—if you listen for it.

It is your life.

It is all the things you've forgotten. It's everything this breakneck world has diverted your attention from.

It's been a few years now, and still, when I'm down with the blues, I look for the white beam. I listen for a riff and I tune out the static. I watch for that brilliant light, because everything that is in *it*, is in me.

Porter Fox is getting his MFA in creative writing from the New School in New York City. He is also at work on his first collection of short stories.

67 The Creepy Blues

TAYLOR DAYNE

The blues . . . are creepy.

They come around the corners.

A hike in nature, a walk in a quiet neighborhood, looking at the clouds and trees, admiring the beauty around you, a stillness outside the walls of your own mind.

That usually does the trick.

Taylor Dayne's versatile and powerful voice has gained recognition in multiple genres from pop, dance, and rock to adult contemporary. Taylor's unique vocal style has garnered two double-platinum albums, *Tell It to My Heart* and *Can't Fight Fate*, as well as the gold *Soul Dancing*. Visit her at www.taylordayne.com.

68   The Writing Blues

JEFFREY A. CARVER

Music is my best antidote for the blues. I'm a writer by trade, and I get pretty low when my writing isn't going well. That's how closely I identify my life with my work. I'm not saying that's a good thing, but there it is.

Writing, far from being glamorous, is often a painful process. The dull ache of staring and staring at the glowing screen when the thoughts aren't coming (this can go on for days, weeks, months), or the sharp, recurring certainty: Face it, kid, you've written every original sentence you're going to write. You're on a downhill grade with retreads, and the treads are shaking loose!

In this state of mind, I'm not open to hearing from my kids what a great writer I am (*of course* they think that), or reminders from my wife (what does *she* know?) that I've felt like this midway through every book I've written, and they all came out pretty well, didn't they?

Yes, they did. But so what? That was then. This is now.

I write science fiction stories set among the stars. I sometimes forget that I do this because I *love* the cosmos, the stars and nebulas, the galaxies, and all of the mysterious things and beings that await our discovery there. If I can't wander among the stars in person, then by God, I'm going to do it in my stories. I tell myself: Remember? This is why you write. Why you struggle to get the stories out. Because stories matter. Stories help us know who we are, where we came from, where we're going. Stories come from a deep well that's common to us all.

The trick is reaching deeper into the well. Prayer is one way. Reading. Dreaming. And music. For me, John Williams's music for the *Star Wars* movies. The Moody Blues from their cosmic period. Cream. (Does that date me? I could go on.) Music reawakens the dreams.

And it chases away the blues.

And if that doesn't work? That's when I say the hell with it, the kids are coming home from school. By the time I've immersed myself in *their* world for a while (and really, what could matter more?), I've generally forgotten for at least a while that I was feeling down in the first place.

Jeffrey A. Carver is the author of fourteen science fiction novels, most recently *Eternity's End,* which was nominated for the Nebula Award. A native of Ohio, he now lives outside Boston with his wife and daughters. You can read some of his shorter work and learn more about his books at www.starrigger.net.

69 The Rainy Blues

DELBERT MCCLINTON

The best way to beat the blues is to not let other people do your thinking for you. And the best way for a songwriter to describe beating the blues is in a song. Here's the way I put it, in "Watchin' the Rain."

> *Spent a lot of time in the past*
> *Kissin' other people's ass.*
> *Now I'm where I wanna be,*
> *Sittin' here watchin' the rain.*

Grammy-winning blues rocker Delbert McClinton started out performing with such legends as Sonny Boy Williamson, Jimmy Reed, Big Joe Turner, and Howlin' Wolf. While he is known for his own chart-topping releases such as "Givin' It Up for Your Love," Delbert McClinton is a noted writer, having penned many hits, including "Two More Bottles of Wine" for Emmylou Harris. Visit his website at www.delbert.com.

70 The Sheltering Blues

LAURA GILPIN

Maybe because I was born in Wisconsin and grew up in Indiana and Alabama, trees have always been part of my native landscape. I can live without mountains, oceans, and lakes, but I cannot live without trees. I think of trees as ancient grandmothers, sheltering and beneficent. Their metaphors have shaped my life: resiliency through the harshest seasons, flexibility, strength, a willingness to let go, being firmly rooted, knowing where they stand. Trees have a mythic presence in my life, giving me perspective in dark times. They seem almost wise to me. This poem was written especially for this book, and in gratitude to trees.

Trees

When I am sad, when I am pulled tight
into a hardened knot of pain or pity,
I try to find a way to open myself
by thinking of trees. Of course,
it is difficult to think of something so full
and radiant as a tree when I am small

and pulled into a dark closed shell. Sometimes
it is possible only to think of trees
I have known since childhood,
the willow arching over my earliest memories,
the magnolia of my grandmother's backyard,
the oak that has stood all my life by the edge of the road.
Not that it is easy to imagine something rising up, tall,
although trees too were once small and knotted
and buried in darkness.

Maybe that is why trees are so comfortable in the shadows,
why darkness gathers around them, is drawn to them,
pooling beneath them, collecting on the undersides of leaves,
between the fingers of their branches. Maybe
that is why trees seek out darkness with their roots,
feeling into the deepest, softest parts of the earth,
to pull from the darkness the sweetness,
and from that sweetness draw the strength to look up,
to reach out, to grow towards the light.

Laura Gilpin is a poet and a nurse. She is the author of *The Hocus-Pocus of the Universe,* which won the Walt Whitman Award in 1976. She also received a fellowship from the National Endowment for the Arts. She lives in Fairhope, Alabama, and is completing her second book of poetry.

TANYA TUCKER   137

71 The Starry Night Blues

JOHN LAPPEN

When I was just a punk, I'd beat the blues by swilling as much cold German beer as I could get my hot little hands on, and stuffing my face with thin-crust slices of sausage-and-mushroom pizza.

Now that I'm all grown up, I still love to swill cold German beer and eat thin-crust slices of sausage-and-mushroom pizza. But these days I beat the blues by remembering precious thoughts from my childhood. The one I refer to most is when my beautiful, sweet mother and I would sit on the front porch of our house in Appleton, Wisconsin, and count the stars in the sky. We'd have long talks that only a young son and his mother could have and, before we went into the house, she'd always give me a big hug and a kiss, and tell me how much she loved me.

I never fail to think of her when I look at the nighttime starry sky. Those warm thoughts never fail to kick ass on the blues.

John Lappen is a thirty-two-year veteran of the music industry. Some of the acts he's been privileged to be involved with include The Doors, Eric Burdon and the Animals, Deep Purple, Tommy James, the Monkees, Paul Kantner of Jefferson Airplane, Joan Jett, the Allman Brothers, the Turtles, and countless others. Based in Los Angeles, Lappen is also a music critic for *The Hollywood Reporter*.

72 The Vietnam Blues

SHAD MESHAD

When a dark day arrives in my life for some unknown reason, I think back to times when I was in some dark places. I will usually start with my tour in Vietnam as a young army captain, working with soldiers with psychological stress from the war. In my mind nothing could be worse than to be there in the middle of this conflict with death and dying around you every day of your tour.

I remember singing the words to a current hit song over and over, as did so many of the soldiers, about wanting to "get outta this place." We wanted to get out alive. But it was just a mantra, and we were never quite sure if it would work. Your soul was in the darkest place on earth, and you prayed that it would end one day, and your life would return to a safer and a more normal life in America, or "the world," as we called it. Home Sweet Home.

Well, I did return home, and I continued my work as a therapist with the young men from Vietnam who were returning for a new shot at life. The world. I will never forget that situation, and that God allowed me to return and live! The feeling of being given a new chance at a life without horror is forever tattooed in my memory. Nothing can ever be that bad again for me in my lifetime.

So, I just recall that situation, when I thought I would never get out of "that place," and I thank God I have come home to live a great life, one after that nightmare as a soldier in 'Nam. Nothing can hold me in the dark when I reflect on that for just a moment. It's the only good thing that came out of Vietnam for me, except for my buddies who also made it home, and who stay in touch with me to this day. The blues just ain't got a chance when I reflect on all of this.

Shad Meshad is president and founder of the National Veterans Foundation. You can visit the foundation's website at www.nvf.org.

73 Honky-tonk, Muzik, and the Blues

BIG & RICH

JOHN RICH: On the rare occasion that I get the blues, I find that, man, extremely loud honky-tonk with a well-stocked bar and a lot of pretty girls goes a long way to improving my state of mind. If that doesn't work, I listen to Frank Sinatra and drink expensive bottles of red wine.

BIG KENNY: To me, it always depends on what shade of blue I am. Am I dark blue or light blue? The remedies may include passionate love or a bottle of fine Cabernet with friends. Muzik seems to bring me to a better place. And, of course, I never forget the number one cure-all: love!

John Rich began collaborating with Kenny Alphin (Big Kenny) in 1998, putting together weekly songwriter sessions at Nashville's Pub of Love that were quickly dubbed the "Muzik Mafia." In 2003 Alphin and Rich's song "She's a Butterfly" was recorded by Martina McBride, and the duo subsequently landed a record deal of their own with Warner Bros. Records. Big & Rich debuted in February 2004 with the single "Wild West Show," from the CD *Horse of a Different Color*. With the release of "Save a Horse, Ride a Cowboy," Big & Rich established themselves as leaders of Nashville's new wave. You can visit their website at www.bigandrich.com.

74 The Yorkshire Blues

CHRIS SIMPSON

Everybody gets the blues in some shape or form from time to time. Mostly, it is an intense feeling of sadness; a desolation of the soul that knows no permanent remedy, arriving sometimes unexpectedly and departing just as mysteriously. There is no known cure, but music helps. Add to that the comfort and understanding of friendships, and the blues will vacate the premises and move on.

Yesterday I felt as if the whole world in all its brilliance and heartbreak lay heavy on my shoulders. I couldn't tell why, but every view seemed to be uphill on rocky ground. I had the blues.

Then tonight, here in this village of 184 souls, I left my office by the little hill river, where I had been stagnating for much of the day. The great hills lay in serried ranks along the northern horizon, where the sky was hung with stars. The gas clouds of the Milky Way were blazing in the celestial landscape directly above my head, scaling me down to something tiny and insignificant. Yet, I had a sense of being at one with the Creator of it all. I could feel, as so many times before, the blues losing their grip against such a backdrop. How can you be sad when the whole of creation is spinning above your head?

As I walked under the blanket of night up the path to the cottage, the wind sifted through pines by the river, a sound like the scend of the sea on some forgotten shore. The cottage was built of stone eleven years before the Pilgrim fathers landed in America. It has great oak beams, and sculpted friezes above the stone-flagged floors, and a fireplace that is big enough to sit in. I stand with my back to the logs spitting in the hearth and, once again, the peace and wisdom of the old house reaches down across the centuries. The cottage has seen it all. I think of the countless souls who have lived, hoped, and dreamed under this roof. Often, with the candle-light playing tricks, I see "them" watching and hear the undercurrent of their voices.

Slowly, but surely, the blues lets go and heads into retreat. Tomorrow is another day.

There is a profound comfort in that.

Chris Simpson was born in North Yorkshire, England. Both his parents were from Nidderdale, his father's side of the family descending from border reivers who came down into the northern dales in previous centuries. Chris's life on the road has slowed very little since 1969, when he first formed the group Magna Carta.

75 The Lawn Mower Blues

LITTLE RICHARD

When life gets you down, just keep this in mind: The grass may look greener on the other side. But believe me, it's just as hard to cut!

Named the originator, emancipator, and architect of rock 'n' roll, Little Richard was among the first inductees in the Rock and Roll Hall of Fame. His other honors include a star on the world-renowned Hollywood Walk of Fame, the Lifetime Achievement Award from the National Academy of Recording Arts and Sciences, the Rhythm & Blues Foundation's prestigious Pioneer Award, the American Music Awards' distinguished Award of Merit, and induction into the NAACP Image Awards' Hall of Fame. You can visit his website at www.littlerichard.com.

76 The Map-Crease Blues

DAVID LOGAN

I grew up in the crease of a map. Jacksonville is so centrally located in Illinois that the atlas folds right over on top of us, like a stapled equator. Most people passing through tend to look to the Shawnee Hills in the southern reaches, or Chicago to the north. But we locals walk the line drawn right across the middle in a region known for two mighty things: Abraham Lincoln and damn good soil. Some folks here work the land, and the rest feed heartily from it. It is a landscape flattened by nature, one that defines its inhabitants in lifestyle and trade. We are weather-conscious farmers and swing-shift laborers. We are the sons and daughters of the heartland.

My dad is a man to be admired for the love he gave unendingly, and the sweat he shed for his family. He worked hard, long hours running a grader and putting in roads we rarely used. I didn't grow up to build roads. I started mowing lawns and trimming trees six days a week, sometimes seven. I worked golf courses, striping grass in alternating patterns and designs. I soon found a silence in the noise of a chain saw, a place of peace that can help a man get his mind off his blues.

But growing up deep in the map crease, I became restless.

Once I realized how badly I wanted out, I didn't know how to do it. I had never done it before. So I found a group of friends with the same lack of belonging and no way out. We drank whiskey along the airport road while we watched single-engine planes leave and then return again. We shaved our heads or grew our hair long, learned guitar, read Salinger, and hung out in the pool hall. I tried to beat away the blues with a constant buzz, hiding out in cornfields, along farm roads, or under isolated bridges. It was the only escape I could find until my restlessness consumed me and I'd finally had enough.

I packed up my dog, grabbed my guitar, and moved to the mountains of northern Arizona. I took little with me, but tried to leave the blues behind. I was ready to start over, a whole new life beyond the flats, a new life where corn didn't grow, where whitetail deer became elk, and where the San Francisco Peaks sat framed in my window. But I quickly learned that it's not so easy to leave a suitcase of blues behind. The things I tried to outrun were waiting for me in Arizona. Before I knew it, I was back to mowing grass and trimming trees, and I was still lost in the same buzz, only worse.

I finally returned to Illinois a few years later with no intention of staying. Just passing through, I'd tell myself. But to fall in love with home a second time around is enough to shed those blues on most days. I've been back in the map crease now for six years, and though I may still be just passing through, I'm in no big hurry to leave this time. It's good to be among family again. And I've met up with a lot of old friends, made a lot of new friends, and made a lot of good love.

Nowadays, when I get the blues, I pick up and use those roads built by men like my father. Nothing feels so good as the possibilities in a full tank of gas. And when I've been gone long enough, whether it's been a month or a day, I follow the crease in the map. That's the road that leads back home.

David Logan is a tree trimmer and adjunct professor in Springfield, Illinois. He is at work on his first novel.

77 The Unbeatable Blues

KRIS KRISTOFFERSON

I don't beat the blues; the blues beats me.
   Daily.
   Like a drum.

Grammy-winning Nashville Songwriter Hall of Fame member Kris Kristofferson is one of music's premier writer/artists. His award-winning hits include "Me and Bobby McGee," "For the Good Times," "Sunday Morning Coming Down," "Help Me Make It Through the Night," "One Day at a Time," and "Why Me." He has starred in over forty-four films and recorded in excess of twenty-five albums. In 2004, Kris was inducted into the Country Music Hall of Fame.

78 Dissecting the Blues

PAUL GAHLINGER

Being a slow learner, it took me the better part of a half century to figure out how to beat the blues. The solution turned out to be simple, really, and has no doubt been obvious to most people throughout the ages. For me, however, it was a revelation. The solution, to put it plainly, is to break down the problem into the smallest components possible, and then look at each of these individually. My immediate discovery is always that each little part of the problem is not that bad. Most of the pieces are no more than a pestering nuisance, or annoyances that are easily fixed. It's the total package that's so discouraging.

I see this in my clinical practice almost every day. For example, a man is devastated by his newly diagnosed prostate cancer. He is faced with impotence, incontinence, and his own mortality, each of which has a freightload of issues ranging from self-worth to public image. So depression, on the heels of prostate cancer, is understandable. Or is it? When you break down each of these issues, it turns out that every one of them is a relatively manageable challenge, a concern that has several remedies, or a dilemma that presents a number of practical solutions. None of them individually are worthy of depression.

For some reason, the blues always come wrapped in layers of health, relationships, work, finances, and other issues. It is never just one distinct problem. So the answer, I finally realized, is to dissect the miserable situation into tiny components, and get on with doing something to fix at least one of them.

There is a large cadre of investigators who study just what it means to be happy. This is what the students of happiness have found: family, pets, community, doing good work, and so on, make you happy. But everyone already knows that. I'm more interested in the neurological component.

Our notion of the brain is roughly that described by René Descartes in 1694. He said the body communicates with the brain by nerves, like a bell ringer pulling on a cord to ring the bell. And, as Quasimodo knew, the bell can also ring the ringer. That notion was elaborated to the recent view of the brain as an intricate computer: a hundred billion nerves, each of them connected with up to two hundred thousand others. It gets mind-bogglingly complex. Like a computer, happiness is programmed, sort of, and if you could fix the circuit, you could fix the lack-of-happiness problem.

Some neurophysiologists have explored the basis of happiness in the brain. The latest view of the brain differs from this image of a fixed wiring diagram. It turns out that nerves change in response to stimuli and their environment. Signals sent to the brain are not just received; they actually alter the brain. That explains the effect of exercise or playing with puppies—the physical act also affects the brain. Signals entirely within the brain change it, too. A happy thought, amazingly, causes a physical change. So simply by *pretending* to be happy, you can truly become happy. The happiness ability of the brain is like a muscle—work it long and hard enough and you can become the Schwarzenegger of ecstasy.

So, if feeling blue is a matter of chemistry, and we can change brain chemistry by sheer thought alone, then it seems logical to stop feeling blue just by deciding to do so.

But if that fails, I personally reach for the ultimate weapon: a pint of Ben & Jerry's New York Super Fudge Chunk.

Paul M. Gahlinger, M.D., Ph.D., M.P.H., FACOEM, is the author of many books, among them the recently published *Illegal Drugs: A Complete Guide to Their History, Chemistry, Use and Abuse*. He is currently an adjunct professor in the Faculty of Medicine, University of Utah, Salt Lake City.

79 The Friendly Blues

BILLY BOB THORNTON

I don't try to beat the blues. I just try to get through it.

I figure every time I get through another spell, it makes me stronger.

The blues almost seem like an old friend to me. It's a good time to create.

Academy Award-winning writer, actor, and director Billy Bob Thornton first received critical acclaim in 1992 for his performance in *One False Move*. He wrote and directed *Sling Blade*, which won him an Oscar for Best Adapted Screenplay and a nomination as Best Actor. He is also an accomplished songwriter, musician, and singer and has released two CDs, *Edge of the World* and *Private Radio*.

80 Fly-Fishing Through the Blues

MACYE LAVINDER MAHER

I live in the most scenic, sensual, extreme place—Jackson Hole, Wyoming. There's mountain healing all around. But I'm sensitive. I need more than mountains.

To lose the blues I go fly-fishing. I find a secret Rocky Mountain stream and watch as my fly floats naturally down an easy current. My husband, Alex, is somewhere nearby, but out of sight around the bend. I love the quiet space.

All of a sudden the fly line zings. The weight of something animated followed by a silver streak forces me to realize the necessity of living in the moment to land this fish. Letting out line as the wild thing dashes upstream, I stumble on slick river rock. Yet the crazy bend in the rod tells me something remains connected. Heartily, I'm reeling in the empty slack of the fly line, reeling until a trout emerges. I run my hands through the water and hold this fascinating creature. The Snake River cutthroat trout wiggles furiously to show me its health and independence. I watch the mouth chomping dry air, admire the bold ginger slash on the jaw, a cutthroat's unmistakable defining feature.

It is time now to let it go. There is no room left for anything dismal when reality can be this fantastic and rejuvenating. We are as resilient as we want to be.

Macye Lavinder Maher is a freelance writer and angler of international experience. She manages the ranch brokerage team at Live Water Properties, LLC as a day job.

81 Outriding/Outplaying the Blues

BRET MICHAELS

Nothing cures the blues and wakes up my soul more than a long ride on my Harley, followed by several hours spent playing my acoustic guitar.

Poison lead singer Bret Michaels has written ten Top 40 singles, including the hit "Every Rose Has Its Thorn." Poison sold over 20 million records. Despite this overwhelming success, Michaels understands the blues. He has suffered from juvenile diabetes since the age of six. For thirty-four years, the singer has taken four insulin injections and eight blood tests each day to maintain his health and survive the disease. You can visit his website at www.bretmichaels.com.

82 The Ageless Blues

PATSI BALE COX

When I was in college I was my sorority's eccentric scholarship chairman and roomed with Bonnie Partin, the equally eccentric campus beauty. One time some foolish girl asked us: "How do you two get along so well? Bonnie, you're so pretty, and, Patsi, you're so smart!"

Bonnie smiled and said: "We're roommates. That means she knows I'm not really that pretty, and I know she's not really that smart."

We got along famously.

For Bonnie and me, unworthy men meant "the blues," and we had only one way to beat 'em—figuratively, of course, and always on the weekend because we both really were serious history students.

When one of us found herself circling the drain over a love gone wrong, we came back to our apartment on a Friday afternoon, locked the door, took the phone off the hook, dressed in faux 1940s lounge pajamas, which we'd found at a perfectly fabulous yard sale the previous fall, applied massive amounts of eye makeup, opened a bottle of Johnnie Walker

Black Label, and smoked Marlboros in rhinestone holders while listening to Ray Charles records.

On Sunday night we clicked our glasses to the last of the scotch and toasted the weasel of the week. Then, on Monday morning, we dressed in smiles and sorority blazers for the Panhellenic Council meeting.

Nearly four decades later, the blues are complicated, a much more formidable adversary. These days it takes more than cocktails and Ray Charles to chase them away. Sometimes I catch them sneaking into my house and I attack with righteous anger. I grab the blues by the throat, choke them, stomp on them, and kick them right through the door again.

Other times I just sit there frozen, hoping they grow weary of me and find their own way out.

Former magazine editor Patsi Bale Cox has written many celebrity books, including *Nickel Dreams* with Tanya Tucker, *Still Woman Enough* with Loretta Lynn, Jenny Jones's *My Life*, Tony Orlando's *Halfway to Paradise*, and Ralph Emery's *The View from Nashville* and *Fifty Years Down a Country Road*. She is cowriter of *A Country Music Christmas*, and is currently working with Wynonna Judd on her memoir.

83 The Texas Hold 'Em Blues

DANIEL NEGREANU

When I get the blues, I try to focus on all that is right with my life. The truth is, you can decide to be in a good mood if you really want to, so when I catch myself pouting, I give myself a kick in the ass. "Don't be such a wimp. Things could be worse. A lot worse."

Personally, I'd feel too guilty if I whined or was depressed. My life has been pretty easy compared to most, so complaining about my Lexus getting a flat tire, or losing an unlucky hand at poker, would be a slap in the face to those less fortunate.

So I beat the blues by not letting the blues beat me.

Daniel Negreanu is considered one of the best poker players in the world. In 2004 alone, he was named ESPN Player of the Year, *Card Player*'s Player of the Year, Champion of the Year, and runner-up for the World Poker Tour Player of the Year. Originally from Toronto, Canada, Daniel writes a biweekly column for *Card Player* magazine. His articles can be accessed through his personal website, www.fullcontactpoker.com.

84 The Sunday Blues

CATHIE PELLETIER

No wonder Picasso painted everything blue for three years, during his period of great melancholy. The color red could never capture sadness. That's why we don't call this down feeling "the reds."

I might get the blues on any given day, but I can always count on the Sunday blues, which have afflicted me since I was a child. I think it's because I came from a tiny town at the end of the road in woodsy northern Maine where Sundays were so slow. This was at a time when I wanted life to go very fast. Folks tended to sit around all day in their best clothes, and the whole town went to bed early, leaving just a few of us diehards still awake. Mondays meant school again, and they also meant that Mama dragged her wringer washer out into the middle of the kitchen floor and did the wash. Piles of clothing. The smell of detergent. And it always seemed to rain on wash days. So part of the Sunday blues was because I dreaded Mondays. I hated going to school and missed a lot of days.

When I became a teenager, I'd often ride around on Sunday nights with a late-night friend, drinking a few beers and just killing time in some old car with a great radio and a full tank of gas. *Turn at the Catholic church, drive back down the twisty road that follows the river, turn at the grocery store, don't hit the gas pumps, drive back up to the church, turn again.* For hours. When that was over, I'd lie in bed and listen to the hits winging up from WPTR, down in Boston, which we could pick up even that far north. Tommy James and the Shondells, James Taylor, Simon and Garfunkel, the Monkees, Gary Puckett and the Union Gap.

Now that Mama is gone, she's become a part of my Sunday blues, for I miss her beyond words—her blue eyes, her laughter, her big Sunday dinners. When I go back home to Maine, the porch lights aren't on and waiting for me, as they used to be. Daddy tries to remember, but Mama never forgot to turn on the porch lights. When I was a child, standing at the edge of a cold woods, icy skates slung over my shoulder, I'd often feel that same old sadness. But I knew I'd be safe if I could see in the distance the warm yellow lights of our house. It would mean everyone I loved was still safe.

The damn Sunday blues. God, I dread them. But I'm older now, and just wise enough to realize that a light at the end of the tunnel might be the train. So when I see the blues coming, I try to stay busy at my computer, or by walking the dogs along the creek. Nature can heal us all, if we let it.

But if that doesn't work, I put on my brown felt hat and open a bottle of red wine. I turn on all the lights in the house, so it will appear as if everyone I ever loved and lost is safe again, and home. If the weather permits, I sit by an outside fire and look up at the stars. The early Egyptians thought the stars were tiny lanterns carried by the gods. That makes me smile. Then I think of how, on this fragile ball called Earth, I managed to find my husband, Tom, and that he loves me no matter what. I remind myself how lucky I am to have such good friends. How lucky I was to have two wonderful parents.

Now I'm grounded again, so it's time to play the songs that make me sad. (That's the Irish side of my heart, thanks to Mama.) I put on "Magnolia" by J. J. Cale, or "Sad Old Wintry Feeling" by Jesse Winchester, or "The Dutchman" by Steve Goodman, or "Good Ole Boys Like Me" by Bob McDill, or "Live Forever" by Billy Joe Shaver, or "Our Town" by Iris Dement, or "Mary" by Patti Griffith, until I finally get to Carly Simon's "Like a River." I let the words in those songs tear my guts out.

There's a reverse kind of power in doing that, as if the blues didn't expect it. But the best defense is a good offense, so I've learned to meet the blues head on.

Here's a thought for all of us with the blues to remember: Picasso's blue period was immediately followed by his rose period.

Cathie Pelletier is the author of six novels under her own name, which includes *The Funeral Makers, Beaming Sonny Home,* and *The Weight of Winter,* which won the New England Book Award for fiction. Under the pseudonym of K. C. McKinnon she has written two novels, *Dancing at the Harvest Moon,* which was translated into nineteen languages and was a CBS TV film, and *Candles on Bay Street,* which was translated into ten languages. Pelletier has had songs recorded by the Glaser Brothers, the Texas Tornados, and David Byrne. Visit her at www.kcmckinnon.com.

85 Outjumping the Blues

CHARLES BARKLEY

I got one word for the blues: rebound.

Charles Barkley is one of only four NBA players, with Kareem Abdul-Jabbar, Wilt Chamberlain, and Karl Malone, to have more than twenty-three thousand points, twelve thousand rebounds, and four thousand assists. He was named NBA All-Star eleven times and won two Olympic Gold Medals (1992 and 1996). Nicknamed "the Round Mound of Rebound," he is a regular studio analyst on *Inside the NBA*.

86 The Swamp Blues

CARL HILEMAN

I have had the blues in predictable cycles for as long as I can remember. When I was younger, I didn't know what they were or didn't think about it much. Those blue times were just another way of looking at life. A certain somber intensity. A calmness where I looked inward, instead of outward. But if it weren't for the blues, life would be a gentle ride. Long ascending and descending curves. No jagged edges. No spikes and pits.

I *need* the blues.

The highs in my life are worth the lows. As an artist, I am more productive on either end of the cycle. I usually paint, play the guitar, write songs, or spend time alone in nature. I walk in the nearby wooded hills overlooking the Mississippi River. And then on to the Cache bottom swamps, which are remnants of the Cache River. Swamps always feel and smell like the blues, as if maybe that's where the blues were born.

But I always know when it's time to quit "the blue world." That's when I seek out my friends and family. It's the knowledge that they are a positive part of my life that reminds me it's time to leave the swamps and those seductive blues behind.

Carl Hileman's most recent collection of photos and text is *Cows: A Rumination,* published by Emmis Books in October 2004. An artist, photographer, and songwriter, Hileman lives in a home he built for himself on the border of the Shawnee National Forest in southern Illinois. He currently operates his own art studio dedicated to painting, photography, and graphic design. He is the photographer for *A Country Music Christmas* (Crown) and illustrator of *The Christmas Note,* a children's book by Grand Ole Opry star Skeeter Davis. His illustrations are included in K. C. McKinnon's *Dancing at the Harvest Moon.* Visit him at www.carlhileman.com.

87 Blues for Sale

ROBERT WESTWOOD

To say I had an idyllic childhood is almost downplaying it. And maybe that's another reason I am known to get the blues now and then. My mother was from the Machris family, which meant her father was head of Wilshire Oil Company, the largest of the independent oil producers. My dad grew up working for his father at the Westbrook Carburetor and Alternator Shop in Hollywood. They made a perfect couple. He became the leading ace fighter pilot of the 13th Air Force. They nicknamed him "the Hollywood Ace." I still have a recording of my father on the Dick Powell and Lucille Ball shows. He was killed leading a strike against Japanese shipping in Makassar Harbor, Celebes. My mother also died young, at the age of thirty-four. I was raised by Aunt Katy, my mom's sister, who happened to be a friend of Ava Gardner.

When I became a young man and expressed a desire to study bullfighting, it was Ava Gardner who took me in as a houseguest and introduced me to some top fighters. It's not a bad thing having Ava Gardner as your landlady.

At my twenty-first birthday party, held at Romanoff's in Beverly Hills, I was waiting for midnight to roll around. When

I officially turned twenty-one, the head of my grandmother's bank drove over to deliver me a check for *one million* bucks. As a part of my trust fund, it was to be one of many to come. I remember thinking, God, life is going to be easy.

Over the course of the next twenty or so years, I would own a four-star restaurant in Beverly Hills as well as a hotel in Santa Barbara. I had always loved and played music, so in the 1970s I started a management company with a good friend. We even managed Albert Collins, a great bluesman. For a long time it was fast cars, fast boats, fast planes, and fast women. Then, when I was forty-five, my best friend and partner swindled me out of everything. I woke up one day and realized I was damn near broke. But what hurt more was the loss of a friend's trust. I felt as though I'd been stabbed in my heart.

Blues? I couldn't begin to tell you about my blues.

One smart decision I made was to buy a Ramirez guitar while I was in Spain. I started playing it hard and writing songs harder. Now when I sing, "I've been broken, I've been busted, by the people that I've trusted," you can bet your sweet derriere I know what I'm singing about. But despite it all, music makes me smile. And I have never been too far from my guitar.

Today, I have emphysema. That's the breaks. I live on an all-wood sailboat. It's quiet in the evenings. No television to distract or annoy. It's just me, the sound of water lapping against the boat, and my same old Ramirez guitar, my good and constant friend for over forty years. The emphysema doesn't stop me and my band from playing at some pretty cool L.A. clubs. I just drag the O_2 bottle over one shoulder and the guitar over the other. I kick-start my '67 Triumph motor-cycle and make my way through L.A. traffic to get to the club.

Here's what I've learned: Money can be nice. It can even be necessary for a lot of things. But you can't buy away the blues. And money didn't buy my parents long and fruitful lives. Instead, concentrate on the things that you already own, and that no one can take from you, whether you've got money or not: Music. Sunsets. Loyal friends. Joy. Inner peace. That's the expensive stuff.

Robert Westbrook lives on his sailboat in Marina del Rey, California. Visit him at www.geocities.com/westbrookmusic.

88 The Blues Is the Blues

JERRY LEE LEWIS

I grew up on the blues.
I was influenced by the blues.
I love the blues.
So when I *get* the blues, I just play 'em.

Rock and country legend Jerry Lee Lewis signed with Sun Records in 1956, and within a year two releases—"Whole Lotta Shakin' Going On" and "Great Balls of Fire"—ensured his position as one of the founders of rock 'n' roll. In 1986, Jerry Lee was among the first artists to be inducted into the Rock and Roll Hall of Fame. Visit his website at www.jerryleelewis.com.

89 The Unemployed Blues

JAY HECKMAN

Some people call it hard times and some call it the blues. A couple of years ago I called it "being over fifty and out of work." All of a sudden all my thoughts and fears were centered on one thing: I was of no value to anyone.

When you start to think that way, the blues will kick you down the stairs and laugh while you fall. Don't get me wrong. I knew life had ups and downs, good times and bad. I knew that the blues are part of everyone's life. But when I lost a job in midlife, a bone-chilling panic hit me. I started focusing on the negative, on the ominous prospect of my life playing out as some kind of bad script. And because I allowed it to do so, the blues started spiraling down, down, down until they started to define me.

I had to turn things around, and the way I started was by admitting to myself that I needed to talk to people I trusted. I had to come right out and admit that I was down, worried, scared.

Was it hard to be honest about my over-fifty job fears? Sure. It's hard to admit you're feeling weak, to ask for advice and help. It's hard to say, "Have you heard of anything?" You always think they'll be coming to *you*.

But here's the truth: When you start to be honest with yourself and others, when you start to open up, then something else shows up—hope. Hope is vital when you're facing down the blues. I'm not talking about false hope. I'm talking about the kind of hope that happens with honesty and trust and friendship, the kind of hope that comes from a friend reminding you that experience *does* count.

So the bottom line for me is this: Don't ever shut your friends out of your blues.

Hope and friends. Even the blues can't beat that.

Jay Heckman is now an account manager for Outdoor Lighting Perspectives in Phoenix, Arizona. He has recently written his first novel. Visit him at www.hidemesundown.com.

90 The Sidecar Blues

WALLY LAMB

For novelists—moody sorts, more often than not—embracing the blues rather than chasing them away is part of the equation by which a book gets written. You suffer alongside your characters. (Picture the book's protagonist gripping the motorcycle's handlebars, the angst-ridden author seated in the sidecar.) But on those days when beating the blues becomes an absolute necessity, I dispatch gloom in these ways:

1. I hit the floor and hang out with little kids, the gigglier the better. Peekaboo, funny faces, pony rides (neighing is good for the soul), pratfalls: the more I behave in ways which I imagine might unnerve erudite literary prize judges, the better I feel.

2. I work with my writing students at a maximum-security women's prison. Tears fall during every session, but there's always the music of communal laughter, too. For the inmate, humor can be a powerful antidote to feelings of shame, regret, and hopelessness. Sometimes I'm heavyhearted when I arrive at the prison, but I always feel uplifted by

the time I leave, having gotten back as well as given.

3. I put gospel music in the CD player. Although I've been uplifted by the likes of Lyle Lovett ("I'm Gonna Wait"), Tom Waits ("Come on Up to the House"), and Billy Joel ("The River of Dreams"), I find that resounding vocal choirs, played LOUDLY, work best. On the worst days, cranking up the Abyssinian Baptist Choir's "Said I Wasn't Gonna Tell Nobody," or the Edwin Hawkins Singers' "Oh, Happy Day" can vanquish the blues.

Wally Lamb's novels, *She's Come Undone* and *I Know This Much Is True*, were number one *New York Times* bestsellers, *New York Times Book Review* "Notable Books of the Year," and Oprah's Book Club selections. He is currently the volunteer facilitator of a writing workshop for incarcerated women at Connecticut's York Correctional Institution. From this program has come *Couldn't Keep It to Myself: Testimonies from Our Imprisoned Sisters*, an anthology of autobiographical essays by incarcerated women.

91 The Scam Letter Blues

BRAD CHRISTENSEN

I've got an interactive hobby that blends creativity and humor with a vigilante spirit to help me beat the blues. It's spam-scammer baiting, or turning the tables on e-mail fraudsters who promise you a share of a multimillion-dollar fortune in exchange for payment of fees to transfer the money out of their country, usually Nigeria.

Instead of deleting the scammers' offers, I reply with feigned interest, beginning e-mail journeys they will truly regret. Clouded by greed, they have actually believed I was the proprietor of a fast-food restaurant specializing in pickle tacos and E. coli, an elderly executive who demanded meetings on nude beaches (to "ensure transparency in business affairs"), and the inventor of the BarfLog home security device ("burns in the fireplace while one is away, producing an olfactory blanket of protection no thief would dare invade!"). Once I posed as an eccentric birdwatcher on the prowl for long-extinct flying pterosaurs. The would-be scammer actually claimed such creatures could be found "in abundance" in Ghana.

Often I pretend to book a flight and ask the scammer to meet me at the airport in the wee morning hours. Sometimes the scammer will actually agree to fly to another country to meet me, but I've always got an excuse for not showing up ("Sorry, but I got on the wrong plane and ended up in Lisbon, North Dakota, not Lisbon, Portugal"). As you can see, my hobby not only relieves my blues, it gives the bad guys a serious case of the stuff!

Nigerian e-mail scams have proliferated in recent years, making them an international annoyance in which victims' dollar losses are listed in the hundreds of millions in the United States alone. But nobody has been harmed more than the honest, hardworking Nigerians whose international reputation and prospects for economic development have been poisoned by the actions of a few.

It is my hope that my hobby will spread the word about this fraud and hasten its elimination. After all, humor may be the most powerful weapon in mankind's arsenal—and a damn good way to beat the blues.

Brad Christensen is a Wisconsin transplant who lives in Peoria, Arizona. He is a journalism graduate who has written professionally for more than twenty-five years, first as a newspaper reporter and editor, then with the Arizona Health Department. He is currently public relations manager for an international engineering company. You can visit his website at www.quatloos.com/brad_christensen.

92 The Boring Blues

KINKY FRIEDMAN

My old favorite way to chase the blues was trying to commit suicide by jumping through a ceiling fan. Since that has proved unsuccessful and costly, I now invite people over and pretend I'm listening to their problems for hours.

As soon as my house pests have departed, so have the blues! Try it. It works.

In the 1970s, Kinky Friedman turned his unique brand of satire into country music stardom with his band, the Texas Jewboys. After becoming a music icon, Kinky penned novels, including *Greenwich Killing Time, Armadillos & Old Lace, Elvis, Jesus & Coca-Cola, The Prisoner of Vandam Street, Curse of the Missing Puppet Head,* and *'Scuse Me While I Whip This Out: Reflections on Country Singers, Presidents, and Other Troublemakers.* You can visit his website at www.kinkyfriedman.com.

93 The Four-Legged Rescue Blues

NANCY PARKER SIMONS

Nothing brings me down faster than abandoned animals. That's why my husband, Tony, and I (with the help of my cousin Kinky Friedman) founded Utopia Animal Rescue Ranch, near Medina, Texas. My daily "no-fail" recipe to keep the blues at bay is cooking up cheese-and-garlic quesadillas for our fifty-plus rescued dogs, with Tony helping.

Over a year ago I read a holistic animal book that extolled the many benefits of garlic. For example, garlic helps remove stress, kills internal parasites, and even repels fleas from dogs (not to mention masking the smell of Kinky's cigars). After discovering this information, I embarked on coming up with the perfect recipe that was loaded with garlic for our mutti-grees. After several failed recipes and kitchen fiascos, garlic cheese quesadillas won hands down! Our dogs absolutely love them, and we can easily mass-produce these tasty treats in under forty-five minutes, if the Kinkster is not helping us. (If Kinky helps, I add one additional hour for preparation time and take two aspirin.)

Our next governor (hopefully) of the great state of Texas, Kinky Friedman (our Gandhi-like figure at the Utopia Animal Rescue Ranch), has officially named my quesadilla recipe,

Cousin Nancy's Flea-Be-Gone Finger Food!

INGREDIENTS

Small flour tortillas
Shredded cheese (any kind)
Jar of crushed garlic
(Leather gloves optional)

Take one small flour tortilla and sprinkle about one tablespoon of shredded cheese on it. Next, add two tablespoons of crushed garlic and spread evenly over the tortilla. Cover with another tortilla and place in a hot skillet. Brown both sides until cheese is melted. After doing this fifty times, run outside and feed your fifty dogs.

Nancy Parker Simons runs Utopia Animal Rescue. Visit her at www. utopiarescue.com.

94 The Positive Blues

ROCKY BLIER

As a young man I learned a very valuable lesson: I have a choice. Every morning when I wake up I have a choice in how I want to spend my day. I have a choice in how I want to feel, how I treat people, and what my disposition will be. For most of my life I have been very positive. It's just easier. It takes a lot of energy to be negative. That outlook got me through Vietnam, two years of rehab, and twelve years of getting the crap beat out of me in the NFL.

But on those rare occasions when I allow myself to wallow in self-pity and beat myself up for being human, all I have to do to beat the blues is remind myself that I am not in a fox-hole in Vietnam, or a bed in the hospital, or looking into the eyes of a 250-pound linebacker who wants to hurt me. Now I look into the eyes of my two little girls, who are six and five years old, and I see all the hope, love, and wonderment they possess. It reminds me that I have a choice. They need me. Life is good.

In 1968, Notre Dame All-American halfback Rocky Blier became a member of the Pittsburgh Steelers, selected 417th out of 441 football players drafted in the NFL. Sportswriters didn't give him much of a chance at professional football glory, which seemed a moot point later that year, when he was drafted to serve in Vietnam. Blier returned home with a forty-percent disability after being severely wounded in the leg and foot. Despite all odds, Blier showed up for spring training with the Steelers. He went on to become one of the Steelers' most valuable running backs and win four Super Bowl rings.

95 Aldo and the Blues

HAL KANT

Every poker player is familiar with the gut-wrenching despair of watching as one unfortunate card hits the table and all your chips are pushed to another player.

At the Amarillo Slim Super Bowl of Poker tournament, held at Caesars Palace, I was particularly depressed at being knocked out of the Championship No-Limit Poker event. I had won the Championship Omaha Pot Limit tournament at the World Series of Poker, had come in second in the Limit and No-Limit Hold 'Em events, and had won several other important events at various venues. I felt I had a reputation to uphold, and I had just failed.

My gloom deepened when my checkout was delayed by a cashier screwup. Added to this, my private plane was grounded with an engine problem and I had to fly home commercial. With each passing moment, as I waited for the bellman, I became a bit more irritated. Finally he appeared, a small man in his sixties with a smile on his face and an eagerness to talk.

His name was Aldo, he told me, as he picked up my bag and followed me out of the hotel, chatting all the way. I remained hostile and mute.

"Where you from?" he finally asked.

"New York," I told him, still surly, hoping that would be the end of it.

"No kidding," he said. "I'm from New York, too. The Bronx."

As it turned out, Aldo had grown up just a few blocks from where I did. As we walked to the limo he told me of the friends we had in common from our adjoining ghettos, friends who had suffered early tragedies. Several of them had been shot to death.

"I been here at Caesars Palace for twenty years now," Aldo told me. "This is the best job I ever had."

Aldo, seven years my senior, was thrilled with his life as a bellman. He saw the honor and the satisfaction in a job well done. Yet here I was being a dejected jerk over a game of cards.

So now, whenever I bemoan small losses and inconveniences, I simply remember Aldo, and that clears away my blues in an instant.

Hal Kant is an international entertainment industry and corporate lawyer who represented, along with other celebrity clients, the Grateful Dead for over thirty years.

96 Burning Down the Blues

BLAKE SHELTON

The quickest way for an entertainer to get the blues is to make a little money, squander it, and wind up broke when the career cools off. So when I started to earn some money, I decided to invest in something I knew would last: land. I ended up buying a good-size farm with many old structures on it—barns, old houses, things like that.

But there's another thing about the blues. Sometimes when you feel your life getting cluttered, or your emotions confused, it's good to clear out the old. Worrying about that old, falling-down barn, in particular, would bring me down every so often. So one day I drove my tractor out to that barn, razed it, and set it on fire. I guess you could say that's "burning down the blues."

In 2001, Blake Shelton's debut, "Austin," spent five weeks at number one. Then, in early 2002 the Hoyt Axton–penned "Ol' Red" was released with a vivid video. It soared to the top of the charts and drove the Blake Shelton CD to gold status. You can visit his website at www.blakeshelton.com.

97 The Blue Heaven Blues

JOSÉ EBER

When I get the blues, I take off my cowboy hat and put on a gray fedora with a black hatband and deep dark sunglasses. I go out and buy myself a new pair of shoes and try to walk away the blues. Eventually, I find myself walking along Sunset Boulevard, handing out money to the people standing on the corner in rags and torn sneakers. It wakes me up, and I smack myself in the face for having the audacity to have the blues in the first place.

I have a friend who writes when he has the blues. He writes gorgeous lyrics, and he says that in the expression of them, he transcends the blues into a state of what he calls Blue Heaven. This friend said that one evening he was lifted up out of the blues by the haunting music of the great jazz vocalist Jimmy Scott. In turn, he was propelled to write a song inspired by the effect that Jimmy had on him in that moment.

Many of us are elevated by a certain sound or feeling we get from a musical moment or a scene in a film, from some simple event that transports us to a pure state of feeling. It's a good way to deal with blues, creatively, putting thoughts on paper. And it's something anyone can do, whether it ends up as poetry, lyrics, or just some thoughts recorded at random.

I'd like to share with you my friend's description of what happened in one of those blue moments, when he was moved by the music of Jimmy Scott. I think you will feel something from this lyric, something that goes right to the heart of the blues and pulls you, too, into that state of Blue Heaven.

Midnight with Jimmy Scott

Tonight Jimmy Scott's voice swirls like smoke through this room
Drunkenly quiet
And perfectly tuned
And Jimmy Scott's soul
Tumbles slow through the air

Perfectly haunted
And perfectly clear
And Jimmy Scott's pain is
so sharp it fits
Through the cracks of sorrow and out into bliss

Some people never fit in this world
But they contain the Seven Heavens
It drips from their lips
It sighs through their life
Their wrinkles as they age are maps of all time

Just let him in your ears
You'll find Jimmy Scott
For all that he is
And more so for all that he's not.

There's rain on the window
In the middle of the night
There's music in the room
Jimmy Scott slow dancing
In waterfront light

And you,
You catch a glimpse of your heart
Before it was ever harmed
Strong as the Twin Towers
Before they were bombed
Like the first memory you have
Of being charmed

Like the heartbreak that never healed
When you were assured it would be gone
Like a song that gets you through the blues till dawn
And Jimmy Scott continues singing
Through this night
And life continues on . . .

One of the most celebrated figures in the world of beauty, José Eber is known for the styles he created for Farrah Fawcett, Elizabeth Taylor, Cher, Tanya Tucker, and other stars. In addition to his flagship salon in Beverly Hills, Eber owns nine salons in the United States and a hair care line. Visit his website at www.joseeberatelier.com.

98 Escaping the Blues

RAY "BOOM BOOM" MANCINI

Whenever I get the blues, I like to sit alone someplace: my home, a café, a park. I smoke a cigar, have a cup of coffee, and think. I try to take my mind to a different place. This is an exercise I learned when I was fighting.

During training camp, I learned that whenever negative thoughts threaten to take over, you must train yourself to escape to a comfort zone, a place of refuge in your mind. It has to be a place where only tranquil feelings and positive thoughts flow. It's your emotional rescue. You must flush out the negativity with the positive energy that you get from thinking of happy times when you felt warm and loved.

It is a process, but with continued training of the mind, you'll get there quicker and quicker.

Ray Mancini's father, Lenny, was a top contender for a world championship in boxing before being wounded in World War II. In 1978, Lenny's son Ray turned pro and lived out his father's dreams. Known as "Boom Boom" for his whirlwind style, Mancini won the Lightweight World Championship on May 8, 1982, in a two-minute-and-fifty-four-second bout with Arturo Frias. Following his career in the ring, Boom Boom Mancini went on to become an actor and public speaker.

99   The Corner of Joy and Peace Blues

TAMMY FAYE MESSNER

I have learned that everything in life is a choice. We make choices every hour of every day. We start making those choices the minute we wake up in the morning.

You may wake up feeling awful, so your excuse all day long is, "I woke up on the wrong side of the bed!" It will not only ruin your day, but the day of everyone who has to be around you. Or, you can wake up in that same bed, feel the same way, but make a different choice: You can choose to turn a negative into a positive.

My life has been filled with disappointment, hurt, humiliation, and loss. I could have chosen to live in all that garbage and today I could be an angry, bitter woman. But I chose to forgive those who had hurt me, disappointed me, humiliated me, and caused great loss in my life. I made a choice not to carry all that "stuff" around on my back, day after day, week after week, year after year. It was far too heavy for me to carry. I unbuckled the heavy load, I laid it down before God, and mentally walked away from it. And I never looked back.

There is nothing we can do about what happened yesterday. It's like an egg that is broken. It can never be put back together again. Today is a new day. Choose to make it the best day you ever had. Not one of us is guaranteed tomorrow! Do I ever get the blues? Of course! Do I ever have a pity party? *No!* Pity parties and feeling sorry for ourselves have *never* gotten anyone anywhere. When you fall, pick yourself up, dust yourself off, and start all over again!

I have two verses from the Bible that really help chase away the blues. They will help you, too, if you will believe what they say. Here they are:

Romans 8:28: For we know that all things work together for good to those that love the Lord and to those that are called according to His purpose.

Thessalonians 5:18: In everything give thanks, for this is the will of God in Christ Jesus concerning you.

Wow! How can I stay blue with promises like that?! I have learned that life is what you make it. The choice is YOURS! I refuse to live on Blue Avenue; I want to live on the corner of Peace and Joy. You see, it's not the circumstances in life that destroy you; it's your ATTITUDE toward the circumstances!

You can make it! Don't ever give up!

Tammy Faye and Jim Bakker founded the world's largest Christian network, called the PTL Television Network, in Charlotte, North Carolina. For twenty-five years, she cohosted the show with Jim Bakker. Tammy Faye has recorded over twenty-five albums and written four books, *I Gotta Be Me*, *Run Towards the Roar*, *Tammy: Telling It My Way*, and *I Will Survive*. She is an ordained minister, now married to Roe Messner, and she often speaks at churches, conferences, and conventions.

100 The Tucker Children Beat the Blues

PRESLEY, AGE 15: When I feel a little down, I can always bring myself up with a song: pop, rock, country, I love it all.

GRAYSON, AGE 13: Consider me gone fishin' . . .

LAYLA, AGE 5: Popsicle.

Printed in the United States
By Bookmasters